for Leather

A straightforward guide to leather:

origins - manufacture - applications

by
Paul McElheron
and
Mike Mirams

Published by:

THE SCANDINAVIAN
BUSINESS ACADEMY
Making a difference

Published in 2015 by:

The Scandinavian Business Academy
Digevej 11, Brøns, 6780 Skærbæk, Denmark

CVR number: 29790280

Copyright © Paul McElheron & Michael Mirams 2015

Paul McElheron and Michael Mirams have asserted their rights under the Copyright, Designs and Patents Act 1988 to be identified as the authors of this work.

All rights reserved. No part of this publication may be reproduced, stored in a retrieval system or transmitted, in any form or by any means, without the publisher's prior permission in writing.

This book is sold subject to the condition that it shall not, by way of trade or otherwise, be lent, resold, hired out or otherwise circulated without the publisher's prior consent in any form of binding or cover other than that in which it is published and without a similar condition, including this condition, being imposed on the subsequent purchaser.

Every responsible effort has been made to trace copyright holders of material reproduced in this book, but if there are any that have been inadvertently overlooked the publishers would be glad to hear from them.

ISBN-13: 978-1517314200

ISBN-10: 1517314208

L FOR LEATHER - CONTENTS

INTRODUCTION   9

ACKNOWLEDGEMENTS   11

CHAPTER 1, PRESENTING THE CASE FOR LEATHER   13

What Is (and is not) leather?   14
Industries working in tandem
What makes leather unique?
The great smell of leather
Leather substitutes
Biofabrication – a sustainable alternative to leather production?
Leather applications   18
Leather for furniture
Leather for footwear
Leather for clothing
Leather gloves
Other goods
Etched leather artwork
Leather's occasional bad press   22
The environmental impact of raising animals for meat
The impact of the leather industry on the environment
The use of chromium (chrome) in leather tanning
A little about chrome
Animal welfare issues associated with the meat industry
What is being done to promote animal welfare
Leather versus 'fast fashion'   29
The global leather industry   31
How big is the leather industry?
Where is leather produced, and where does it go?
Where does the best leather originate?
The typical leather tannery business model.

CHAPTER 2, THE WORLD'S SECOND OLDEST PROFESSION?   37

Leather and our ancestors   37
Origins of leather
Prehistoric
More recent evidence
The development of the leather-making process through the ages   40
The leather-making process

Medieval tanning methods
Vegetable tanning
Parchment and vellum
Modern methods of leather-making
Chrome tanning discovered   **45**

CHAPTER 3, TYPES OF LEATHER   **51**

The structure of leather   **51**
Cattle (bovine) leather   **53**
Calfskin
Domestic sheep (ovine) leather   **55**
The surface of sheep leather
Goat or kid (caprine) leather   **57**
Pigskin (porcine) leather   **59**
The surface of pig skin

CHAPTER 4, MORE EXOTIC TYPES OF LEATHER   **63**

Horse leather   **63**
Kangaroo leather   **64**
Deer skin   **66**
Camel leather   **67**
Ostrich leather   **67**
Chicken leather   **68**
Reptile skins   **69**
Snakes
Lizards
Crocodile and alligator leather
The difference between crocodile and alligator skins
Fake crocodile leather
Amphibians   **75**
Frog skin
Fish   **76**
Stingrays (shagreen)
Eel skin
Sharkskin
Human leather   **81**
Shrunken heads
In conclusion   **83**

CHAPTER 5, LEATHER FINISHES   **87**

    Aniline finish   **88**
       How to identify aniline leathers
    Semi-aniline finish   **90**
    Pigmented full grain leather   **91**
    Corrected grain leather   **93**
    Finished splits   **93**
    Suede   **94**
    Nubuck   **95**
       How to identify nubucks
    Embossed leather   **95**
    Pull-up leather (waxy or oil pull-up)   **96**
    Dry milled leather   **97**
    Antique grain (two-tone leather)   **98**
    Laminated leather, PU leather   **98**
    Patent leather   **99**
    Glazed finish   **100**
    Other finish effects   **100**
    Recap of terms   **100**

CHAPTER 6, HOW LEATHER IS MADE   **103**

    Setting the scene: do-it-yourself tanning   **103**
    How does leather tanning work?   **104**
    Vegetable tanning   **106**
       The vegetable tanning process
    Mineral tanning   **110**
       Chromium (chrome) tanning
    Chrome tanning - an overview   **111**
       Beamhouse processes
       Re-tanning (finishing)
    Chrome tanning processes in detail   **112**
       Beamhouse operations
       Chrome re-tanning (finishing) operations
    Combination tanning   **118**
       Comparison between vegetable and chrome tanned leather
       How to differentiate between vegetable and chrome tanned leather
    Other mineral tannages   **120**
    Other Tanning Materials   **121**

CHAPTER 7, LEATHER QUALITY   **125**

The perception of 'quality'   **125**
Source
Utilisation
Conformance to specifications
Grading
Consumer expectations
Restricted substances   **127**
Measuring leather characteristics   **128**

CHAPTER 8, BUYING LEATHER   **131**

A consumer's guide to buying leather   **131**
Buying leather furniture
Questions to ask
Inspecting the leather
Sofa construction
Purchasing leather garments
What to look for
Buying leather footwear
Commercial leather purchase   **136**
The hobbyist or small scale designer of leather goods
Small to medium sized enterprises
Sourcing suppliers
A model supplier selection and approval process   **139**
Dealing with suppliers   **142**

GLOSSARY OF LEATHER-RELATED TERMS   **147**

INDEX   **151**

INTRODUCTION

This book is a compilation of the training materials we have put together over several years as part of our teaching 'Understanding Leather' to business and design students at VIA Design, part of VIA University College in Denmark, and other colleges and corporations.

The research for the book has included the literature and information on issues surrounding leather, interviews with experts within the leather industry including tanners (the people who actually make leather) and people who deal in leather including agents, wholesalers and retailers of leather products. There has been much interesting research relating to leather carried out over the years covering the history of leather and the science relating to its production. We have tried to encapsulate this into a concise guide useful for anyone who works with leather, as a purchaser or in sales, for designers using leather or leather products; in fact for anyone who has a general interest in leather as a material.

One of the challenges in researching for this book was the realisation that there are many variations in opinions and points of view about leather and its applications, each of which we explore in some detail within the chapters that follow, including animal rights and welfare issues (and the often hazy boundary between the two), leather's occasional 'bad press' and the need for the media to create sensational reports. Articles are frequently uninformed, inaccurate and confusing. Additionally, poor practices are prevalent in many areas of the world where leather is made, and there are issues related to working conditions and pollution control.

The leather industry generally takes the view that it is making good use of a valuable bi-product of the meat industry that would otherwise go to waste. Not only do they have respect for the raw material and the animals from which it is derived, but most people involved in the making and distribution of leather and leather goods behave responsibly concerning matters of protecting the environment and have a genuine passion for the product. Paul worked in the polymer industry for many years and did not come across many people passionate about plastics, but you meet people in the leather industry with a passion for their material all the time - they believe they are making a sustainable product of great use and value. We are sure that Stephen Tierney, editor of World Leather, speaks for many in the industry when he states: "By the time a tanner gets his or her hands on a hide, there is nothing to be done for the animal except, we would argue, show respect and gratitude to it by, post-mortem, transforming its hide into the natural, flexible, durable, breathable, sensual, versatile, beautiful, prestigious material that is leather. Also, simple logic tells us that the better the animal has been treated beforehand, the better the quality of the hide will be, so tanners support and speak up about good treatment of animals prior to slaughter" (Tierney, 2014).

In our research for this book we discovered that there are areas of the world where animal welfare and tannery effluent are major problems. In terms of tannery waste, bad practice here seems to be due to ignorance, poor control, corruption, practices within the industry, and not least, economics. If you are one of a cluster of 100 tanneries and the other 99 get away with dumping untreated waste into the river rather than taking on the expense and trouble to treat it – well it is obvious what will happen. However, in this area there are signs of improvements in countries such as China and India where there are increasing government initiatives being taken to deal with tannery waste.

We would go a step further and say that the leather industry has the potential to reposition itself as a solution to environmental problems rather than an industry that contributes to them. We know of no other uses for the vast volume of animal hides and skins generated from the livestock and meat industries which, if they were not converted into something useful, would be an environmental problem.

So what qualifies us to write about leather and what is our purpose? We are not employed in the leather industry and we have no affiliations with animal rights groups. We do have a great interest in leather. We have over 40 years' combined experience of working alongside the leather industry and we support the use of leather for its unique properties, aesthetics and sustainability. While not animal rights activists, we do care passionately about animal welfare and we make the distinction between the two in the book. We have tried to provide an accurate and as balanced a picture as possible concerning leather, both praising good practice and addressing the bad. If we have got anything wrong, please let us know.

Paul McElheron and Mike Mirams, July 2015.

Paul J McElheron is a lecturer and researcher at VIA University College in Denmark where he lectures in leather technology and a range of business subjects. He has authored several books and academic papers. Prior to entering academia Paul held a series of research, technical and commercial positions in the footwear and polymer industries, including 11 years with footwear manufacturer Ecco Sko A/S, where he travelled widely working in shoe factories and tanneries throughout Europe, Asia and South America. Paul is also founder-director of The Scandinavian Business Academy, an organisation providing management training for commercial clients as well as support for skills training initiatives in Asia.

From an engineering background, **Mike Mirams** has been an independent consultant focusing on the improvement of quality and the development of international supply chains in many industries (including leather) for nearly 25 years. Also a published author of books and articles, in more recent times he has been involved in the development of world-class skills training in the leather industry in India.

Paul (left) and Mike during a break from editing "L for Leather" in Summer 2015

ACKNOWLEDGEMENTS

With special thanks to:

VIA Design, The South Tyrol Museum of Archaeology, The International Council of Tanners, Robert Kanigel, Stephen Tierney, Mark Evans, Kobi Levi, Janne Kappel, Mike Redwood, International Union of Leather Technologists & Chemists, World Animal Protection, Museum of Leathercraft, ECCO Sko A/S, Chester Grosvenor Museum, Michael Young of Sørensen Leather, The RSPCA, Marks & Spencer, Exoticleather.biz, The Houghton Library – Harvard University, BLC Leather Technology Centre, J. Hewit & Sons ltd., Bjarne Andersen, (Læderiet), Tarnsjo Tannery, The Museum of Leathercraft, Betty Bevan.

A special thank you to Alexei Patrascu for the illustrations.

Cover inspired by the VENCA Cow, VENCA CRAFT INC.

This book is dedicated to our long-suffering wives, Marianne McElheron and Lesley Mirams, who *nearly* lost faith that it would ever be completed!

CHAPTER 1, PRESENTING THE CASE FOR LEATHER

In this chapter we explore the background of leather as a material and what makes it unique. We look at some common applications for leather as well as some of the more unusual ones. We address leather's occasional bad press, the impact of the leather and tanning industries on the environment and the serious issue of animal welfare. We put some scale to the global leather industry and finish off with a typical tannery business model.

Photo 1.1a; The discovery of Otzi

In September 1991 a German couple, Helmut and Erika Simon, hiking in the Tyrolean Alps, stumbled across a frozen body emerging from a melting glacier. Only the back of the head, bare shoulders and part of the back could be seen protruding through melting ice and at first it was thought they had found a mountaineer who had met with an accident. However, following an investigation at the morgue at Innsbruck, it was subsequently established that the find was actually a mummy, (named 'Otzi' after the valley in which he was found), later estimated to have died around 5,000 years ago.

The South Tyrol Museum of Archaeology's website (www.iceman.it) provides a fascinating documentary of the find, recovery and subsequent research which has being carried on Otzi. The mummified body of Otzi and his possessions provides an interesting snapshot of Copper Age European life and has been extensively investigated. Otzi's body was exceptionally well preserved. He appears to have died in cold, dry weather conditions which essentially freeze-dried his body and once claimed by the glacier he somehow remained in a deep gully that protected him and his possessions from the glacier's crushing force. However what made Otzi especially interesting were his possessions which provided a unique insight into the technology and clothing of the day.

There were many surprises in store for Otzi's investigators. His copper axe changed the timeframe for the copper age by 1000 years, but what is of major interest to us as students of leather is his apparel. His boots which, resembled birds' nests mounted on stiffened deer and bear skin, appeared particularly insubstantial for mountaineering; however a replica pair made from identical materials proved to be extremely comfortable and effective in cold mountain conditions. His clothes were quite sophisticated and included several items made from leather including deer and cow skin, a goat skin cap with bear skin ties, fur

Photo 1.1b; Otzi's 'footwear'

leggings and a loin cloth also made from goat skin. His coat was made of goat skin with clear signs that the inner side had been scrapped and cleaned and the skin had been tanned using fat and smoke, and stitched with animal sinew.

How Otzi came to die high up on a glacier in the Tyrolean Alps was the subject of much speculation, and it was almost ten years after he was found that researchers studying X-rays noticed a flint arrowhead lodged in his left shoulder which is now thought to be the cause of death. Untreated wounds to the Otzi's hands also suggest he had been involved in violent combat shortly prior to his death.

Today, Otzi can be seen in the South Tyrol Museum of Archaeology in Bolzano in northern Italy where he is carefully preserved and displayed, his skin has the colour and look of leather.
You can read more about Otzi, the fascinating story of his find and preservation and view images of Europe's oldest natural mummy on the Museum's website, www.iceman.it. [1]

What is (and is not) leather?

The Cambridge Dictionary provides us with a definition of leather:

"Animal skin, treated in order to preserve it and is used to make shoes, bags, clothes, equipment etc"[2].

Leather is a durable and flexible material created by a process called tanning, which may be carried out at a vast industrial scale or as a cottage industry. Leather is also used for bookbinding, leather wallpaper, and as furniture covering. It is produced in a wide variety of types and styles and is decorated by a wide range of techniques[3].

British Standard BS 2780 gives a more technical definition, describing leather as:

"Hide or skin with its original fibrous structure more or less intact, tanned to be imputrescible".

The hair or wool may or may not have been removed, and the material may have been made from a hide or skin that has been split into layers before or after tanning. BS 2780 also states that the amount of surface coating applied will affect whether the finished material can be described as 'Genuine Leather'; for this to be permitted, the mean thickness of the surface layer must be less than 0.15 millimetres and must not exceed 30 percent of the overall thickness. [4]

BS 2780 rules out bonded leather fibre being described as leather. This is material that has been disintegrated mechanically into fibrous particles, and made into sheets using a binding agent; the key requirement that the original fibrous structure must be intact no longer applying. Bonded 'leather' is often used for making cheap belts and furniture.

Industries working in tandem

The vast majority of leather is a by-product of the meat industry. According to The International Council of Tanners (ICT), the value of an animal's hide is between 5 percent and 15 percent of the carcass value. One could say that the leather industry performs a valuable service in converting what would potentially be a waste product requiring disposal into a useful material – leather for footwear, upholstery, apparel, handbags, wallets, belts, gloves etc. To put this into perspective, according to cattle slaughter statistics, approximately 300 million beef cattle are slaughtered annually worldwide, generating a total hide weight of around 8.75 million tonnes, which, if it were not converted into leather, would remain as organic waste, and it has been claimed that the carbon footprint of disposing of this waste would be greater than that of processing it into leather.[5] If all the products mentioned above were not made out of leather, they would have to be made out of some other material, in all probability textiles or of petrochemical origin, which generate a range of other environmental issues.

The leather industry then operates in parallel with the meat industry, ensuring that the skins of the millions of animal killed for their meat are preserved and converted into the versatile and useful material, leather. Other by-products of meat consumption include fats and blood used in livestock feed, explosives, paints, automobile tyres, foodstuffs, cosmetics and of course pet food. The leather industry in turn works in tandem with the footwear, furniture and automotive industries.

While cows, pigs and goats are generally raised exclusively for their meat and dairy products, and sheep for wool and meat, leather tanners only use the hides when the animals no longer have any use for them. There are exceptions however; ostriches are often raised primarily for their skin and feather value. Snakes, crocodiles and other reptiles are other sources of leather where their meat is not always eaten. However, it must be said that these exceptions represent a small fraction of world leather production.

> The skin of virtually any vertebrate can be processed or tanned to produce leather; however the vast majority (over 98 percent) of the world's leather is from four animals.

Photo 1.2; Leather is a by-product of the meat industry

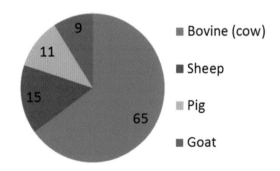

The majority of leather comes from just four kinds of animal (percent)

- Bovine (cow)
- Sheep
- Pig
- Goat

9, 11, 15, 65

What makes leather unique?

What makes this by-product of the meat industry unique? Firstly, leather is a strong material and very hard wearing compared with fabrics. According to furniture experts, leather lasts on average, four to five times longer than fabric coverings. Leather furniture is affordable, hard-wearing and ages well. It reacts readily to temperature change and is easy to maintain.

Leather is breathable and its water vapour permeability makes it the ideal material for use in footwear, as the average pair of feet produces approximately a quarter of a litre of sweat per day. Leather is dust free (beneficial if you are asthmatic) and it is easy to maintain. It is extremely versatile and available in a wide range of colours and attractive finishes.

Photo 1.3; Leather aircraft seats are reputed to last four times as long as fabric equivalents

Leather has a high tensile strength and is very resistant to tearing, flexing and puncture. It also has a unique property - it can be moulded into shapes and still maintain its flexibility and elasticity, (think about the properties of a moulded shoe). It provides good heat insulation, it reacts quickly to body temperature – important for seating comfort in furniture and is generally regarded as being 'warm in winter and cool in summer'.

On top of all this, products made using leather are associated with 'quality' over a range of parameters, including aesthetics, touch, feel, comfort and functionality.

Leather is sustainable and has great longevity. If leather products are well designed and well-crafted they can last for generations. Even leather footwear can last for many years. [6]

The great smell of leather

The smell of leather has been described to us as exotic, luxurious, expensive ('smells of money'), intoxicating and evocative. For most people it's a pleasant smell. The actual smell of leather is a combination of the preserved hide itself and residuals of the many chemicals used in its processing and finishing. It should be easy on the nose and free from any sharp chemical odours. The smell of leather can be reproduced in re-odourants and even perfumes by using a mixture of natural ingredients such as birch oil, juniper and cade oil, vanilla etc., together with a wide range of organic compounds.

Leather Substitutes

The way leather is used has changed over time. Traditionally all footwear was made of leather and all new cars had leather seats. While there is still demand in footwear, automotive applications, apparel etc. leather can and is being replaced by alternative materials. For example, in the 1960s all ski boots were made from leather but today, the content of leather in ski boots is zero. Similarly, in the 1970s and 80s leather was used for almost all sports shoes but now many sports shoes are fully synthetic and have the advantage that they are machine washable. [7]

Perhaps the best way of extolling the virtues of leather is to look at the shortcomings of materials used to substitute for it. Like leather, its substitutes have a long history; fabrics treated with oil to make them resemble leather were around in the 14th century. Leather substitutes are generally used to save cost or for ethical reasons (for example 'vegan' leather), and occasionally to save weight. However, there is really nothing like leather, which, ironically, is why so many attempts have been made to imitate it, usually with limited success.

DuPont spent many millions of dollars trying to market their synthetic leather substitute 'Poromeric' Corfam to the footwear industry. Launched in 1963, DuPont predicted 25 percent of shoes in the US would be made from Corfam by 1983. It had some interesting qualities such as a high gloss finish and it was easy to clean but despite being intensively researched, Corfam was found to be not as flexible or as breathable as leather making it unsuitable for 'comfort' or everyday use. It was also easily confused with plastic, non-breathable alternatives Fashion shoes could have been a possibility but the less expensive material PVC was gaining popularity here. This coupled with the leather industry improving quality and reducing prices resulted in Corfam being withdrawn from the market in 1971 at a cost estimated by DuPont at 80 to 100 million US Dollars.[8] As Robert Kanigel put it, "Corfam was a reminder of the continued resistance and appeal of natural materials in an unnatural world and of the limitations of plastic that had, until then, seemed an implacable force of the future".[9]

Corfam shoes have not quite disappeared entirely; they are still used by some uniformed professions where footwear with a high gloss finish is desirable.

Leather substitutes are used for a range of applications; computer bags and mobile phone covers made from artificial leather are popular and, as long as they are not labelled as leather,

that's fine. Where substitutes really hit problems is in applications where the unique properties of leather are required, which, actually, is most applications! Substitute leathers suffer from a range of limitations compared with the real thing, including limited or no porosity or air permeability, so they accumulate sweat when used in clothing and footwear. They also tend to have an artificial appearance and poor tactile properties. Many also perform badly in a fire situation, burning rapidly and giving off toxic fumes as many are in effect plastic-based materials. There are also biodegradability issues.

Vehicle manufacturer Toyota have recently been using the artificial leather 'Softex' in their RAV4 and Prius V models. Softex is made from thermoplastic PU and has, according to Paul Weisser in an article for Automotive Engineering Magazine, a leather look and feel and good stitching appearance, high breathability, good thermal properties and a tensile strength only slightly lower than leather.[10] Toyota add that Softex has good durability and weighs half as much as leather. However comments from users on the various user forums are a little mixed with some users citing comfort issues relating thermal performance, particularly sweating. Also several users still associate artificial leather with vinyl (PVC), which performed badly when used for seating (Softex is not vinyl). Perhaps leather substitutes still have some way to go not least in public perception terms?

The search for leather alternatives continues however; technology continues to advance and now leather substitutes are made from a wide range of materials including cork, recycled plastics, glazed treated cotton, recycled polyurethane (PU) and polyethylene terephthalate (PET, the plastic used to make water bottles), even recycled cardboard. As long as they are fit for purpose and correctly labelled, no problem, especially if they actually do benefit the environment through recycling.

Some leather substitutes may perform better in one or more selected areas and materials technology moves on continually. However, the combination of leather's unique properties will secure its position as a prestige material in a wide range of applications providing a natural value with a touch of individuality and an alternative to mass produced synthetics.

Biofabrication – a sustainable alternative to leather production?

Andras Forgacs, co-founder and Chief Executive Officer of biomaterials firm Modern Meadows offers an intriguing alternative to current methods of producing meat and leather, which he believes are wasteful, cruel and unsustainable – biofabrication. Biofabrication essentially involves three-dimensional (3D) assembly of meat and leather, and is, according to Forgacs, humane, sustainable and scalable. He cites that we currently maintain a global heard of 60 billion animals to meet the meat, dairy and leather needs of 7 billion people. The size of this global herd will have to reach 100 billion animals to

Is growing leather in the laboratory the future?

meet the needs of an estimated 10 billion people by 2050. He suggests we start with leather, rather than meat, which can be produced using this technology.

Growing leather in this way starts with cells taken from an animal by simple biopsy, isolating them and growing them in a cell culture medium, encouraging them to produce the building block of leather - collagen, spreading it into sheets, layered and subjected to a short chemical process to produce leather. The leather can be 'grown' in the shape of finished products and properties such as transparency, softness, breathability, elasticity, durability can be controlled and even patterns produced.[11] See Andras Forgacs's TED talk for more details and examples of 3D printed leather. Adoption of mass consumer 3D printing, is still some years into our future. If or when the technology does takes off it will be interesting to see what this new material will be referred to – should it be called leather or some new term such as 'bio-leather'?

Leather applications

Leather is an extremely versatile material. Here we look at some of common applications of leather along with some more unusual ones.

Leather for furniture

We have all experienced the feeling of luxury when sinking into a well-constructed leather sofa, the full body support it provides and the great smell of leather. The feel, look and strength of leather make it the ideal material for this type of application producing durable, strong, puncture resistant furniture with unique character. With all but the most specialised leathers, spills can generally be wiped away and scratches are normally easily restored - leather will take a great deal of wear and tear and some leather types develop an attractive patina with age. Leather adjusts to the environment – initially cool to the touch, it adjusts to body temperature within a few seconds. Several airlines, even some of the low cost carriers, choose leather seats over fabric in part due to the more luxurious product but also because leather seats are easier keep clean and last much longer than fabric seats.

Photo 1.4; Leather is an ideal material for sofas

Leather for footwear

Leather is ideal for footwear due to its strength, durability, versatility, good looks and the wide variety of colours and finishes available. It allows the foot to 'breathe' and moulds to fit the wearer's foot, something synthetic leathers are unable to do. It also retains a degree of elasticity, contributing to a level of comfort that only leather can provide.

Leather for clothing

From hot-pants to heavy-duty work wear, the many properties of leather can be readily exploited in the clothing industry. Fine kid leathers are used to make soft and delicate clothing and gloves. Jackets that will last a lifetime are made from aniline and coated

leathers and fine suedes. Remember when men reinforced the elbows of their old sports jackets with leather patches? Well, now it is done as a fashion statement! With the ability to make strong, hardwearing leathers, the material is also suitable for more demanding applications such as motor-cycling apparel, sportswear, and industrial protective work wear.

Leather Gloves

Leather is an ideal material for gloves offering style, durability, warmth and comfort. Leather gloves have been used for centuries for protection from the elements, industrial applications and in battle. From the fifteenth century gloves made from ox, elk, goat, sheep, deer and even dog skin became popular with members of high society. In the 16th to 18th centuries, chicken skin gloves, (apparently so thin they could fit into a walnut shell), were in high demand by ladies who wore them at night in order to keep their hands soft and white,[12] although it appears the gloves were actually a combination of chicken skin and unborn calfskin.[13]

Photo 1.5; This Limerick chicken skin glove (so called after town in Ireland where they were thought to originate) made from chicken and calf skin dates from the early 19th century and is pictured along with a walnut shell in which they were sometimes presented.

Other goods.

A wide range of accessories - belts, wallets, sports equipment, briefcases, handbags, the list of uses for this versatile and natural material is endless. Let's look at some of the more unusual, creative and original applications for leather that we have come across.

Etched leather artwork

Artist Mark Evans from Snowdonia in Wales creates art out of large cowhides. He 'paints' with a blade, with great precision, etching and carving, often removing as little as a tenth of a millimetre of leather at a time. The incisions create shading and tones as a suede beneath the surface is gradually revealed. He calls his work 'micro sculpture', each piece can take months to complete. Mark discovered the technique while trying to remove a blood stain off a new leather jacket. Scratching through the blood created an etched 'nap'. Mark honed his 'micro-sculpture' technique over the years and says of his medium of leather that it's masculine but also feminine and sensual. It has its own evocative aroma and was once a living thing and in a plastic, synthetic, digital world, leather is authentic. To see more of Mark's incredible art work visit www.markevansart.com.

Photo 1.6; Mark Evans' artwork

Kobi Levi

Freelance footwear designer Kobi Levi is known for his amusing, creative and innovative shoe styles which combine the essence of the everyday object expressed as shoes; intended to challenge our definition of design, art and fashion. The shoe is Kobi's canvas for these wearable sculptures which have received world-wide attention; one of his

Photo 1.7; Kobi Levi's 'banana' shoes

designs, a double boot, features in the Lady Gaga video, 'Born this Way'. Kobi's designs are hand-made at his studio in limited and exclusive editions. Prices are in the 1,500 - 3,000 US Dollar price range. To see more of Kobi's thought provoking creations visit www.kobilevidesign.com.

Photo 1.8; Janne Kappel's woman in the chair

Janne Kappel

Danish artist Janne Kappel's work illustrates the versatility of leather. In the example shown here, Janne has formed a figure of a woman using leather and merged the figure into the classic chair designed by Arne Jacobsen. Janne tells us that her inspiration for the piece came when she was sitting opposite a woman in her dentist's waiting room. The woman was clearly nervous about the prospect of visiting the dentist and her body language suggested she was trying to 'melt into her chair'.

Leather's occasional bad press

The environmental and social impact of leather and leather production has been the subject of much discussion. The main issues revolve around the environmental impact of raising animals for meat, the impact of the leather industry on the environment, animal welfare issues associated with the leather and meat industries and the use of chrome in leather tanning.

In the words of the International Council of Tanners, "The reputation of the leather industry across the centuries could best be described as one of tolerated usefulness with a wonderful end product".[14] The output is the versatile, unique material leather, with thousands of uses that are highly valued by most people (the average person will have four leather items with them at any one time, watchstrap, wallet/purse, belt and shoes). However, the process of converting animal hides and skins into leather has, and still does, attract some criticism.

An internet search on leather or tanneries will result in a lot of historical negatives. In the opinion of leather consultant Mike Redwood, part of the reason for this is that no-one is challenging it. No-one talks to the consumer unless they have a negative opinion about leather.[15]

This negative image of leather is something the leather industry is starting to do something about by promoting the positive aspects of leather and leather products. 'Leather Naturally', (www.leathernaturally.org), is an organisation set up to defend the industry, promote leather and its use and educate industries, designers and the buying public. 'Nothing to Hide' is an initiative by World Leather Magazine and comprises a series of articles aimed at countering inaccurate and outdated information about leather and promote knowledge and improve consumers perceptions about the material and the industry as a whole. See www.nothing-to-hide.org.

The environmental impact of raising animals for meat

The meat industry itself attracts criticism and the following statistics are the kind of thing often quoted:

- An area of forest the size of 7 soccer fields is destroyed every minute to make room for cattle.

- Around 200 times the amount of water is required to produce one kilogram of meat than is needed to grow the same amount of wheat.

- 40 kilograms of soya can be produced for the same energy as one kilogram of beef.

- 18 percent of greenhouse gasses are due to livestock farming.

There are also ethical and animal husbandry issues that attract attention. A discussion about the ethics of consuming meat and the effects of the meat industry is beyond the scope of this book; however the rise of factory farming and reduced sense of husbandry, and the environmental effects of raising meat are a concern for many, and animal welfare should be a concern for us all. The reality though is that meat consumption has seen a significant increase worldwide over the last forty years, and so leather is going to be with us for the foreseeable future - in fact demand for leather goods remains robust and in some sectors, especially in footwear and automotive, is increasing.

Critics of the meat industry who target the raising of livestock are perhaps ignoring the realities and needs of developing countries. In the poorer economies, domesticated animals, including cattle, pigs, sheep and goats represent a significant proportion of the wealth of the local population.

The impact of the leather industry on the environment.

Let's turn to the issue of pollution associated with leather production. Large amounts of chemicals are involved in the tanning of leather. However, the past 15 years or so have seen tanneries and chemical suppliers make great inroads into more environmentally friendly practices, no doubt driven by increasing legislation and the increased cost of disposing of tannery waste which is often done by land-fill.

The cost of tannery effluent treatment can be as high as five percent of the value of output; the treatment of tannery waste, strict process control, recovery and reuse of water and chemicals, and ways of ensuring that chemicals used end up in the leather and not in the wastewater, are major preoccupations of tanners and chemical suppliers.

Photo 1.9; The modern water treatment plant at Ecco Shoes' tannery in Dongen, Holland

The pollution from leather making comes in several forms.

Water pollution is generated from several tanning processes; soaking, liming and the tanning itself (see chapter 6, How Leather is Made). Large amounts of organic materials are released during tanning. Large quantities of salt are used and lime and sodium sulphate are by-products of the liming process. By no means all chemicals used are absorbed by the hide during processing. Chromium is used in the majority of tanning processes and this can be present in the waste water. Chromium recovery is possible, but not all tanneries do it.

Air pollution ranges from buffing dust to solvents.

Solid waste includes raw hide trimmings and shavings, hair etc. There are uses for these materials as animal feeds and fertilizers, but supply outreaches demand. A particular problem is the sludge from water treatment which needs to be disposed of in special areas where contamination of ground water is avoided. The bottom line is that only 25 percent of the rawhide ends up as finished leather and the use of over 100 chemicals amounts to over 50 percent more by weight than the weight of the hides processed.

The problem of leather's impact on the environment is especially severe in countries where environmental regulations are lax or not enforced, and these tend to be where much leather is made. Tanneries tend to cluster with some cities, for example in India, having hundreds of tanneries discharging thousands of tonnes of untreated tannery waste daily into the environment. The economic benefits of jobs for workers and profits that will presumably benefit society have to be offset against the disease and suffering experienced by those working within the industry and residents living within the vicinity of the leather tannery, not to mention the wildlife. A 2011 report by the Blacksmith Institute estimated that globally, 1.8 million people's health is at risk due to pollution from tanneries.[16]

Photo 1.109; A tannery in Ambur, South India

Making leather with minimal impact on the environment is possible and most countries have clear environmental regulations governing tanneries. However, if enforcement of these regulations is poor or fraudulent, and there is neither customer nor market demand for cleaner production, or the opportunity for upgrading of technical skills and finances, then regulations will be flaunted. It is generally agreed that the cost of non-conformance with emissions regulations must be greater than the costs of conformance if regulations are to be effective. The cost of compliance in most countries has been estimated to be approximately five percent of production costs, relating to two to four percent of turnover, and this in an industry where tannery profit margins can be as little as two to three percent.[17]

The extent to which tanneries conform to regulations depends on the attitude of the owners and directors, legislation and how this is enforced, and the culture of the prevailing business environment. We have encountered many tannery owners and senior managers who believed tannery chemicals were 'safe' just because they were manufactured in Europe. Also many workers and supervisors handle (usually literally) tannery chemicals on a daily basis without any apparent immediate ill effects; a reason therefore that it is claimed to be okay to release them into the environment.

Tannery pollution continues to be a problem in some parts of the world. An example is India's Kanpur, commonly known as the Leather City of the world due to its large cluster of tanneries. These tanneries pump millions of litres of untreated tannery waste daily into the River Ganges. Part of the problem is under regulation and the fact the city's water treatment facility can only deal with half of the tannery effluent produced. In an effort to crack down on polluting tanneries, the Uttar Pradesh Polution Control Board, (UPPCB) has responded by cutting the electricity and water supplies to 98 of Kanpur's 323 operational tanneries. [18]

Corruption plays a part and in countries where government inspections are seen as opportunities for bribe collection, tannery effluent water quality is irrelevant. However, there are signs that the tanning industry is working towards a greener future. Ask any research and development manager in any medium to large sized tannery what they are working on and usually seven or eight of their top ten projects will result in benefits to the environment. Work aimed at reducing the amount of water and chemicals used in tanning, ensuring that chemicals end up in the leather not the waste water, the use of enzymes to replace chemicals, recycling or generating energy from waste, membrane filtration and chemical recovery are constantly on-going. These efforts are driven mainly by economic pressure but also the need and desire to make tanning 'greener'.

In China there have recently been significant improvements in pollution control; the government has provided waste water collection facilities from smaller tanneries so that waste can be treated centrally in large treatment plants. The same is beginning to happen in Southern India.[19]

An often related story in India concerns the tannery owner whose tannery water effluent was sampled by a local government inspector and was characterised by the testing laboratory as 'highly polluted' because the accompanying bribe was deemed to be insufficient. The tannery owner knew there was nothing wrong with the water sample because, by using a little misdirection in the sampling process, he ensured that the actual sample submitted was pure bottled mineral water! Whilst we cannot vouch for the authenticity of this story, it does highlight the problem.

How far can the industry go with 'environmentally friendly' leather? Time will tell. Several green tanning systems which are significantly lower in emissions and require fewer tanning operations are in the advanced stages of development and will presumably find their way into the industry. It must be said though, that irresponsible tanners in countries where environmental regulations are lacking or poorly enforced will continue to pollute the environment as long as this remains a low cost option for them.

In summary, the production of leather does use large quantities of water and chemicals, but according to Stephen Tierney of the International Council of Tanners, pioneering tanners and new technology are making leather tanning increasingly less resource-intensive. [20] The best tanners and those involved in the tannery industry are consistently cutting consumption of

water, chemicals and energy while reducing waste (and in some cases eliminating waste altogether).

Photo 1.11; Effluent treatment at a modern tannery

The use of chromium (chrome) in leather tanning

There is much confusion, debate and inaccurate information concerning the issue of chrome and its use as a tanning agent for leather. Chrome has been used to tan leather since the early 20th century; approximately 85 percent of leather produced today is so-called chrome tanned. (It has been compared to the Windows system in the computer world). Chrome is a highly effective tanning agent producing a flexible leather within days, which is used in a wide range of applications - footwear, clothing and furniture.

A little about chrome

The element chromium exists in a number of states. Chrome metal is used to harden steel and to manufacture stainless steel, alloys and hard corrosion resistant plated surfaces. Chrome 3 (the type used in leather tanning), sometimes referred to as Cr3, Cr III or trivalent chrome, occurs naturally in the environment in rocks, soil and many plants. This form of chrome is present naturally in foodstuffs and is required by the body to metabolise fats and sugars; chrome dietary supplements are even available. Chrome 3 has been used in leather making for over 100 years and has the same relative toxicity as table salt (sodium chloride).[21] Most chromium is used outside the leather industry, mainly for the manufacture of premium steels and in chromium plating. Some tattoo inks contain chrome. Chrome 3 is considered to be safe to use in leather manufacture.

Chrome 6 (hexavalent chrome) is the material that causes the problems as well as much of the bad press around chrome. Chrome 6 is a hazardous material and can be formed when chrome 3 is oxidized. This occurs in the presence of oxygen, extremes of temperature and acidity. Chrome 6 salts are yellow in colour and are classified as carcinogens and allergens and can cause a whole range of other health problems. The 2000 film *Erin Brockovitch* starring Julia Roberts focuses on the health hazard aspects of Chrome 6. Chrome 6 has no effect on the tanning process and is not used in the manufacture of leather.

Digging deeper – really how 'safe' is chrome (chrome 3) and could there be any situations where chrome 6 is present in leather?
There is a large body of evidence supporting the safety of chrome 3 in leather. A study carried out by the International Union of Leather Technologists and Chemists' Societies 'Chromium and Leather Research; A Balanced View of Scientific Facts and Figures'[22] concluded that, although there is the potential at least for the conversion of chrome 3 to chrome 6, there are several factors that prevent this occurring. Firstly leather is a naturally reductive material, which means that it provides the opposite environment to an oxidizing one required for the conversion of chrome 3 to chrome 6. The leather

making processes and conditions required to ensure chrome 6 does not occur in leather are well known to tanners and are followed. The tanning industry takes the potential risk of chrome 6 very seriously, employing specific precautions to prevent the oxidisation of chrome 3; the vast majority of tanners ensure that there is no risk for workers, the environment and leather end users. There are recognized test methods for detecting the presence of chrome 6. All this means that tanners can ensure leather is chrome 6 free. In the European Union legislation is in place that restricts the amount of chrome 6 in leather and in the environment, which is monitored. The levels found have always been insignificant or below the level of detection.[23]
See also chapter 7, Leather Quality, section on Restricted Substances.

Animal welfare issues associated with the meat industry

In terms of animal protection we need to make a distinction between animal welfare and animal rights. People supporting animal welfare are concerned with the humane treatment of animals. They adopt a utilitarian approach and believe that it's morally acceptable to use animals for food and other purposes as long as any suffering is minimized or eliminated.

One approach to animal welfare has been put forward by Professor John Webster who in 2005 defined good animal welfare as encompassing five freedoms: freedom from thirst or hunger, freedom from discomfort, freedom from pain, injury and disease and freedom from fear and distress and freedom to express normal behavior for that species.[24]

Animal welfarists tend to be against such things as foie gras, breeding animals for fur, intensive

The celebrity chef Hugh Fearnly-Whittingstall takes a welfarist approach with his meat manifesto in his River Cottage Meat Book in which he urges readers to consider the animals from which we get our meat – have they been well treated and fed on safe and appropriate foods? Have they been cared for and how can we be sure of that? Hugh further suggests that we buy from a source that can reassure us on these points. [25]

farming and battery chickens. The area of animal welfare is receiving increasing interest from the scientific community, animal welfare organisations, several brands and the general public as awareness increases as well as from legislators. European Union legislation concerning farm animal welfare is regularly redrafted to reflect growing scientific research and cultural factors. New legislation was introduced in 2009 aimed at reducing animal suffering during slaughter and battery cages for laying hens were banned across the EU in 2009. Individual countries also take action to improve animal welfare.

Animal rights supporters take a more extreme view and believe it is morally wrong to exploit animals for any purposes, no matter how humane, and that includes farming and eating them, medical research and even owning pets. They support veganism and abolitionist education. Some animal rights organisations do support animal welfare in the short-term until more radical measures take effect.

The American philosopher Tom Regan in 1983 summarised both positions well when he stated "Animal rights advocates are campaigning for *no cages*, while animal welfarists are campaigning for *bigger cages*."[26]

Few would disagree that all industries that involve animals should practice responsible stewardship of animals and would benefit by being more humane in their treatment of them. Certainly there are some serious issues for the meat and leather industries to consider and which do require attention. The organisation PETA, (People for the Ethical Treatment of Animals), is the largest animal rights organization in the world with over three million members and is an outspoken opponent of, amongst other things, the leather industry. "Leather is just hairless fur" proclaims their website (www.peta.org), and Pamela Anderson can be found there relating a story concerning truckloads of cattle transported under appalling conditions in India to face awful deaths, and the leather going on to make products for the major fashion houses. Actually this is something that author Paul has seen for himself. "On one occasion I observed cattle having collapsed in the back of an open lorry after a long trip without food or water being 'encouraged' to stand by having their tails broken." Clearly this is unacceptable and PETA is right to spotlight genuine cases of animal abuse. However leather is not of course 'just hairless fur'; it is a by-product of the meat industry.

Which countries are associated with good animal welfare practices? World Animal Protection produces an Animal Protection Index based on such factors as laws protecting animals against suffering, their use in farming and captivity, the welfare of wild animals and several other factors. Countries are ranked in several categories A to G (see next page), where A denotes the highest standards and G identifies areas where the greatest improvements are required. Fifty countries are included in the rankings and they can be found on the organisation's interactive website at www.api.worldanimalprotection.org along with the methodology behind the rankings. Here are the rankings for some of the world's highest producing leather countries along with the UK for comparison:

Category	UK	India	China	Vietnam
Formal recognition of animal sentience	A	C	C	E
Support for the Universal Declaration on Animal Welfare	B	D	G	G
Laws against animal suffering	A	C	D	G
Protecting animals in farming	A	C	C	D
Protecting animals in captivity	B	B	C	E
Protecting companion animals	A	B	D	G
Protecting animals ised for draught and recreation	B	C	D	G
Protecting animals used in scientific research	A	B	C	G
Protecting the welfare of wild animals	B	C	D	D
Overall country ranking	A	C	E	F

(Source: Animal Protection Index, www.api.worldanimalprotection.org, accessed 3 May 2015.)

So what can this information be used for? If you are concerned about these things, it gives a hint about which countries are 'kindest' to animals. It is a way of assessing governments commitment (or lack of it) to animal welfare. However, it is often very difficult for consumers to establish country of origin on leather goods. In an ideal world, producers of leather goods would display the origin of their leather on the product. Customers could then demand leather sourced from countries with good animal welfare provision. This *might* lead to governments in countries with a poor record to commit to animal welfare legislation. However, a few factors would work against this. Firstly brands, in an effort to preserve flexibility in their supply chain, may prefer not to specify country of origin. Another is the way the leather industry operates - tanneries in one country (say Italy), may import refrigerated raw hides or semi-finished leather from another country, India for example. The leather could be finished in Italy and be labelled and later exported as 'Italian Leather'.

What is being done to promote animal welfare?

There are many organisations worldwide that promote good animal welfare and husbandry, and many commercial organisations that follow their principles. The animal welfare organisation, The Royal Society for the Prevention of Cruelty to Animals (RSPCA) in the UK runs the annual Good  Business Awards. The RSPCA's stance when it comes to leather is that they are opposed to the inflection of pain and suffering on, or the killing of any animal, in the name of fashion.

The RSPCA offers the following suggestions for companies wishing to implement an ethical skin and leather sourcing policy:

- Implement a policy not to source skins from certain animals because of conservation issues. Ensure that you do not source skins from wild caught/endangered or threatened animals.

- If you are unsure of the source of the leather, do not purchase it or use the skin.

- Always ensure that the leather is obtained as a by-product of the meat industry.

- Implement a monitoring process regarding obtaining leather and leather items to enable traceability from the original source to finished product, ensuring the welfare of the animal at every stage.

- Ensure that the items you stock and sell are clearly labelled to display the following:
  Country of origin
  The species of the animal used
  Whether or not the animal is a by-product of the meat industry.

Further information given to us by the RSPCA when we asked for their approval to reproduce the above is as follows:

"The RSPCA's primary concern with all animal products whether they are meat, leather or other materials is how the animals in question have been treated and what their quality of life has been. It is of particular importance that the animals have been reared, handled, transported and slaughtered in a way which safeguards their welfare at all times.
'If an animal is to be killed for meat we believe there should be as little waste as possible and as much of the animal as possible should be used. Having said this, the rearing and killing of animals solely for producing leather would raise certain ethical questions." [27]

UK retailer Marks and Spencer requires that non-food products are sourced within a framework dictated by its whole business principles on animal welfare and the

sustainable use of wild animal populations. Some features of their animal welfare framework include:

- The company will, as far as possible, only use animal products where the supplier can provide the name of the species – both Latin and common name, also the country or area from which the animal originated.

- Only non-food products that are a by-product of the meat industry will be used.

- The following products will NOT be used in non-food products:
  Endangered species
  Fur
  Karakul (a product of unnatural abortions)
  Leather or skin obtained from live skinning or live boiling

Full details about Marks and Spencer's ethical policy can be found at www.marksandspencer.com/the company.

Leather versus 'Fast Fashion'

Fast Fashion is the term used to express the quick response approach to moving designs from the catwalk to retail rapidly to capture current fashion trends. Fast fashion has become associated with disposable fashion, and fashion brands having many more collections than the traditional two; Spring/Summer and Autumn/Winter. In fact, many fashion houses and retail stores are introducing new styles every week, driving up consumption and being blamed for damage to ecosystems and the increase of toxic greenhouse gases due to production and transportation.

Cotton represents almost half of the fibres used to make clothing worldwide. According to a WWF report 'Cotton Farming', the production of cotton requires a truly massive input of water, and natural rainfall is often insufficient. The run off from the large amounts of pesticides and fertilisers used when growing cotton has been blamed for the destruction of ecosystems and the health of workers both in the industry and living in surrounding areas. [28]

Synthetic materials which make up the other half of fibres used in clothing have a far from clean bill of health. They are made from non-renewable resources, (oil and natural gas). Many are energy and water intensive, for example polyesters, nylon, polypropylene and polyethylene. Their production often involves the use of carcinogenic chemicals and can produce very harmful greenhouse gases, for example the nitrous oxide released during the production of nylon is several hundred times more damaging as a greenhouse gas than CO_2. Synthetic fibres are essentially non-biodegradable with a poor recycling infrastructure.

A strong case can therefore be made for leather as a more sustainable fashion option in that it does come from a sustainable resource - garments are often classic styles that can be worn over many seasons, and leather clothing is certainly not considered disposable in the way that fast fashion items are. Additionally, studies consistently show that the greatest environmental impact of fibre-based clothing is caused by washing following wear, by drying (if not air dried naturally) and ironing. Typically, for fabrics, up to 80 percent of their energy consumption occurs during in-use laundry.[29] Again, leather apparel scores well here as they are not washed, dried or ironed.

So, does the leather industry deserve the bad press that it sometimes attracts? We believe the answer is "no". Leather *is* a bi-product of the meat industry, converting an unavoidable and otherwise problematic product, continuously generated from another industry, into a sustainable and useful material - leather. Alternatives to leather – fibres and materials of petrochemical origin - have their own environmental issues.

In our experience, having visited scores of tanneries throughout Europe and Asia, the vast majority of producers behave in a responsible manner providing employment for millions without risk to workers, users of their products, or their immediate environment. Yes, there are irresponsible producers and we have cited Kanpur as an example, but this is due to ignorance, ineffective controls and lack of infrastructure; factors that affect all industries in these areas. For example, a significant portion of the pollution problems in Kanpur is due to the mis-management of human waste!

Our conclusion therefore is that the majority of the leather processing industry behaves responsibly and complies with social and environmental requirements. However, there is still a minority of producers that ignore social concerns and environmental obligations, and they do great damage to the credibility of the industry; these do attract the sensationalist press and organisations with their own agendas. We believe that it is important that the leather industry emphasises with greater force the positive aspects of leather and leather making, especially their sustainability and environmental responsibility.

The global leather industry

How big is the leather industry?

Leather is one of the world's most widely traded commodities. Estimates put the global trade value of leather at around US$ 100 billion. The world production of leather has been estimated to be 23 billion square feet, (2.14 billion square metres). [5]

Where is leather produced and where does it go?

China is the biggest producer of leather and leather goods but there is significant production in India and several other Asian countries. South America is also a major producer. In Europe, Italy, Spain and Turkey are the primary producers.

Generally, leather production is increasing by 5-20 percent per annum in Asia, Brazil and some African countries. Leather production is decreasing in most European countries by approximately 10 percent per annum, although there are large country variations.

The major centres where raw hides and skins are produced does not always correlate with where leather is produced so raw hides are transported in a chilled or salted condition or in a partially tanned state. For example, Italy produces around 10 percent of the world's finished leather but has only about one percent of the world bovine herd.

Bovine leathers – top six producing regions in order: Far East, Latin America, North America, Europe, Africa, areas of the former USSR.
Sheep & Goat – top 6 producers in order: China, India, Turkey, Russia, Pakistan.
Pig – China is the largest producer by a significant margin followed by the EU and the USA.

A European perspective: According to Eurostat statistics, leather and leather product manufacturing in the European Union employed 549,000 people in 2006 and generated 11.9 billion Euros of value added. The manufacture of footwear was the largest activity within the leather manufacturing sector accounting for about 70 percent of employment and a smaller majority, about 58 percent of value added.

Almost half of all the value added by the European Union's leather manufacturing sector came from Italy, which has over 1400 tanneries.

The top leather producing countries (percent), bovine, sheep, goat and pig. (Source: Miwinyihija, 2014)

China — 30.5
Italy — 9.3
India — 8.6
Brazil — 7.8
Rep of Korea — 6.5
Russia — 5.8
Argentina — 3.4
Mexico — 3.0
Turkey — 2.8
USA — 2.2
Rest of World — 20.0

Footwear production continues to increase, although the amount of leather in footwear is decreasing due to the rise in the use of non-leather materials. According to industry sources, (www.statistica.com), global footwear manufacture was estimated to be 21 billion pairs in 2012. 13.3 billion of these were produced in China of which 10.1 billion pairs were exported. The next largest producer was India, (2.1 million pairs), followed by Brazil (864 million pairs), Vietnam (681 million pairs) then Indonesia (661 million pairs).

> Tanneries in countries like Italy have remained viable in the face of the tanning industry moving to China and developing countries by using creative business models and providing novel and high quality leathers and benefiting from alliances, a good international image and a fashion orientation. [5]

Where does the best leather originate?

The quality of leather is closely related to the living conditions experienced prior to the slaughter of the animal, including its diet, the probability of skin damage, (by scratches, insect damage etc.) and the age at slaughter. The tanning operation also has an influence, especially in terms of consistency.

About 65 percent of all leather is of bovine origin. Climate and animal husbandry account for the fact that the best bovine leather generally comes from developed countries. Cattle from Northern Europe or countries with similar climate and animal husbandry procedures generally have less skin damage than animals that are herded or ranched. According to Bjærne Andersen of The Læderet (a man with over 40 years' experience of leather buying) the 'best' bovine leather is thought to come from Northern Europe due to the above factors. Cows from Switzerland and

southern Germany have nice skin as they are raised outdoors.

Leather from North and South America is regarded as medium quality but good value for money. Hides are often damaged by scratches and brand marks.
Leather from Asia is generally regarded as of the lowest quality. Although there are differences, leathers from Thailand, Indonesia and Vietnam are considered superior to that originating in India (poor living conditions and age at slaughter) and China (poor living conditions).

To make matters more complex, and general statements about source less reliable, leather from animals raised in one country or continent is often exported to another for finishing, and maybe yet another for making into the finished product. A pair of shoes bought on the high street in any city in Europe could well be made in India from leather tanned and finished in Thailand, but which came from a cow raised in the United States of America!

The typical leather tannery business model

Hege Knutzen of the University of Oslo estimates tanning to be a low profit activity.[17] Profit margins are typically two to four percent and so environmental costs are high in relation to profits. This of course explains why some tanneries in poorly regulated parts of the world are reluctant to incur such costs. Despite automation, in developed countries, tanning remains labour-intensive relative to many other industries.

Tanners compete primarily on price and quality (including the reliability to supply on time). Tanneries are mainly in private hands but are members of national tannery associations which

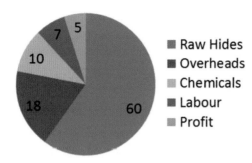

Typical cost breakdown of making leather (percent)

quality and reliability. Many experienced buyers ensure prices are related in part to quality and delivery performance, with discounts of 5 - 10 percent coming into force if deliveries are late or have quality problems.

represent the interests of the tanning industry and offer advice and support. Much of the knowledge is tacit and tanners in some parts of the world (but by no means all) are slow innovators with any developments generally coming from machinery or chemical suppliers or from business client demands.

The cost of leather represents a significant portion of the final product cost, especially in furniture, apparel and footwear, where the cost of the animal's raw hide represents around 50 – 60 percent of the cost of the finished leather. The world-wide supply of leather changes slowly, but demand can alter rapidly as this depends on such things as fashion trends and, significantly, financial issues. The financial crisis in 2008 reduced demand for automotive and furniture leathers considerably which in turn depressed prices for example.

It usually is in both the tannery's and the client's strategic interest to enter long-term partnerships and agreements, keeping the supply chains short. Tanners are particularly keen to be linked with strong international brands; this gives them leverage when negotiating for further business. Margins may well be lower and the hoops that have to be jumped through more numerous, but the associations will help build a reputation for

Chapter 1 References:

1. Hall, S. (2007). [On-line]. *Last History of the Iceman.* National Geographic Magazine. Available at: http://ngm.nationalgeographic.com Accessed: 16/10/ 2014; Bryson, B. (2010). *At Home: a short history of private life.* Doubleday.

2. Cambridge Dictionary Online. (n.d.). Available at: http://dictionary.cambridge.org. Accessed: 03/04/2014.

3. Wikepedia. (2014). [On-line]. *Leather.* Available at: http://en.wikipedia.org. Accessed: 12/12/2014.

4. BSI (1983), *BS2780:1983 + A1:2013,Glossary of Leather Terms.* BSI

5. United Nations Industrial Development Organisation, (UNIDO). (2010). [On-line]. *Future Trends in the World Leather & Leather Products Industry & Trade.* Available at: http://leatherpanel.org. Accessed: 02/06/2015.

6. Redwood, M. (2013). *The concept of the Leather Club and Forum – Mike Redwood.* Available at: https://www.youtube.com/watch?v=X6faS4IsPEs. Accessed: 24/05/2015.

7. UNIDO, (authors: L. Kral, F. Schmel, & J. Buljan). (2014). *The future of leather.* United Nations Industrial Development Organisation.

8. Cashberry. (2006). [On-line]. *Brand Idea Failures: Corfam.* Available at: http://brandfailures.blogspot.dk. Accessed: 09/09/2014.

9. Kanigel, R. (2007). *Faux Real: Genuine Leather and 200 Years of Inspired Fakes.* Joseph Henry Press.

10. Weissler, P. (2013). [On-line]. *New artificial leather gains increasing Toyota acceptance.* Automotive Engineering Magazine. Available at: http://articles.sae.org/11983/. Accessed: 02/11/2013.

11. Forgacs, A. (19 September 2013). [On-line]. *Leather & meat without killing animals.* TEDxMarin. Available on YouTube. https://www.youtube.com/watch?v=7gXq1ml6B1E. Accessed: 02/02/2014.

12. Mahe, Y. (2013). [On-line]. *History of Gloves & their Significance.* Available at: www.fashiointime.org. Accessed 10/11/2014.

13. Ardelie, S. (2013). [On-line]. *Making History Tart & Titillating.* Available at: https://lifetakeslemons.wordpress.com. Accessed: 18/05/2015.

14. International Council of Tanners. (n.d.). [On-line]. http://www.leathercouncil.org. Accessed on various dates.

15. Redwood, M. (2013). *The concept of the Leather Club and Forum – Mike Redwood.* Available at: https://www.youtube.com/watch?v=X6faS4IsPEs. Accessed: 24/05/2015.

16. Blacksmith Institute (2011). *The World's Worst Toxic Pollution Problems.* Blacksmith Institute Report.

17. Knutsen, H. M. (1999). *Leather Tanning, environmental regulations & competitiveness – final report.* Department of Human Geography, University of Oslo.

18. Indian Express (The), February 2, 2015 *Closure Starts for 98 Kanpur Tanneries.* The Indian Express available at www.indianexpress.com, Accessed 17/04/2015.

19. Andersen, B. (2015). Interview with Bjærne Andersen, Læderet, Aarhus held on 4 April 2015.

20. Tierney, S. (2014). *Leather from India*. E-mail dated 08/03/2014.

21. Singh, V. P. (2005). *Metal Toxicity & Tolerance in Plants & Animals*. Sarup & Sons.

22. Tegtmeyer, D. & Kleban, M. (2013). *Chromium and Leather Research: A balanced view of scientific facts and figures*. International Union of Leather Technologists and Chemical Societies.

23. EIPPCD, (European Integrated Pollution Preparation Control Bureau). (2013). *Best Available Technique (BAT) Reference Document for the Tanning of Hides & Skins*. Industrial Emission Directive 2010/75/EU. Available at: http://eippcb.jrc.ec.europa.eu/reference/BRIEF/TAN-A. Accessed: 21/06/2015.

24. Webster, J. (2005). *Animal Welfare: Limping Towards Eden*. Wiley-Blackwell.

25. Fearnley-Whittingstall, H. (2007). *The River Cottage Meat Book*. Hodder & Staughton.

26. Regan, T. (1983).*The Case for Animal Rights*. University of California Press.

27. RSPCA, 15/06/2015, *Leather,* Email to the authors.

28. WWF Report (n.d.) Cotton Farming. Available at http://wwf.panda.org. Accessed: 17/12/2014.

29. Jack, T. (2013). *The dirt on clothes: why washing less is more sustainable.* Available at www.theconversation.com. Accessed : 03/04/2015.

Chapter 1 Photographs:

1.1a & 1.1b. By kind permission of The South Tyrol Museum of Archaeology.

1.2 & 1.10. M G Mirams & P J McElheron.

1.3. Kritchanut, Dreamstime.com.

1.4. John Kasawa, Dreamstime.com.

1.5. By kind permission of The Museum of Leathercraft, Northampton, England.

1.6. By kind permission of Mark Evans.

1.7. By kind permission of Kobi Levi.

1.8. By kind permission of Janne Kappel

1.9 & 1.11. M G Mirams & P J McElheron, by kind permission of Ecco Shoes A/S.

CHAPTER 2, THE WORLD'S SECOND OLDEST PROFESSION?

In this chapter we take a look at the origins of leather making and how it has developed through the ages from stone-age times, through the medieval period to modern day processes.

Leather and our ancestors

The story of Otzi in chapter one of this book reveals that the techniques for converting animal skins into usable leather have a long history. So how long have humans been making and using processed animal hides and skins - leather? Clothing and other leather items degrade rapidly in archaeological terms but there are clues to be found elsewhere. Research based on genetic skin colouration for example indicates humans lost their thick body hair about one million years ago. Professor Nina Jablonski of Pennsylvania State University, in her article entitled 'The Evolution of Skin and Human Skin Colour'[1], suggests this loss of hair was driven by the need to regulate body temperature via sweating. Perhaps loosing body hair encouraged humans to wear animal skins as clothes and use them to build shelters?

Origins of leather

Given our understanding of the climate and populations of several thousand years ago, the vast majority of our ancestors from this period would require protective clothing if they were to survive.

The Stone Age, when the genus *Homo* started to fashion stone tools, covers a period from approximately 3 million years ago until between 8,000 to 4,000 years ago. It seems inconceivable that our earliest ancestors would not throw on an animal skin as protection from the elements at some point. According to the Missouri Museum of Anthropology, the earliest found stone scrapers from Africa, which could have been used to scrape the meat, fat and hair from animal hides, date back 1.6 million years. Acheulean tools, named after the site they were first discovered, St Acheul in France, date back 800,000 years and were thought to be produced by *Homo erectus* (1.9 million to 70,000 years ago).

Our ancestors faced the same challenges that we would do today in that untreated animal hides would either become stiff on drying and so be unwearable, or they would soon rot if kept in a wet or damp state. This would not be a major problem if the skins could be easily replaced, but to make long lasting clothing, some means of preserving the skins would be required.

The production of leather has been described as 'man's first manufacturing process' and there were several materials that could have been used to preserve animal skins close at hand, including the fat and the brains of animals, smoke and vegetable matter (tree bark, leaves, nuts etc.). All these can be used, often in combination, to preserve animal skins.

Photo 2.1;What Otzi may have looked like around 5,000 years ago.

Many indigenous peoples used fat to preserve animal skins. The skins were impregnated with fat, often by rubbing it into the flesh side of the skin and the skin allowed to dry slowly while subjecting it to mechanical action. The fat got in between the collagen fibres in the skin lending the skin a degree of water protection and the collagen fibres remained sufficiently dry to resist bacterial attack.[2]

For small to medium sized mammals, their brains are large enough to help preserve their skin. Brain tanning involves boiling the animal's brain with an appropriate quantity of water, converting this to a paste then applying this paste to the flesh side of the skin that has had all flesh and fat removed and stretched on a wooden frame. The technique is sometimes referred to as 'Indian tanning' as it was a method favoured by native American Indians. Brain tanning can be combined with the smoke from fires. Wood smoke, and particularly that generated from burning green branches and leaves, contains the preservative formaldehyde. Perhaps the discovery of the positive effects of smoking hides was the result of the observation that animal skins used to construct shelters which also covered fires developed advantageous properties such as resistance to rotting when wet.

The Tannery Council of America in its 1937 article 'The Romance of Leather and its Importance to Mankind',[3] describes the leather making processes used by native Indians. The Indians produced leather with excellent softness and pliability with the Crow Indians generally considered to have used the most superior tanning methods with most of the work being done by women. Skins were piled up in a wet state and left to decompose until the hair could be loosened. They were then immersed in a lye (alkaline) solution made from wood ash, then scraped clean on both the flesh and hair sides using bone scrapers. The skins were then rubbed with a mixture composed of the animal's brain and liver then later softened by vigorous rubbing. The final step involved placing the skins in a sealed smoke-filled tent for several days until they became fully cured. This produced a highly serviceable leather; however there is no evidence that native Indians used bark tanning which had been known in Europe for many centuries and brought to America by the new European settlers.

Alternatively, if animals' skins are submerged in water containing the bark and other matter from certain plants the skin will be preserved. *Homo sapiens* (wise man) appeared around 200,000 years ago and had a large brain and the ability to evolve behaviours that helped him survive in difficult conditions. It would therefore seem plausible that, with their thinking ability, they could make the link between chance events such as a hide exposed to green wood smoke or prolonged immersion in water rich in vegetable matter and the skin being preserved against rotting.

Prehistoric

John Pickrell in an article for National Geographic News, 'Toe Bones Reveal World's Earliest Shoe Wearers'[4] cites research carried out by Washington University which found evidence of a weakening of the small toe bones found in 40,000 year old human fossils. The work suggests that wearing supportive footwear results in more delicate small toes. Walking barefoot requires the small toes to flex to achieve traction, promoting sturdy small toe bones. So, weaker small toe bones suggest the use of footwear, and animal skins would have been an obvious choice of materials.

However, the origins of leather making may well be even further back in time. In an article entitled 'Who invented clothes? A Palaeolithic Archaeologist Answers'[5] posted by Becky Wragg Sykes, a Neanderthal (from the period 250,000 to 40,000 years ago) stone tool has been found in Neumark-Nord in Germany with scraps of organic material adhering to it that were soaked in tannin, indicating that Neanderthals were tanning leather using vegetable matter, possibly oak bark, 100,000 years ago. In addition, bone tools now called lissoirs that are used for burnishing leather and making it more water proof have been found at Neanderthal excavation sites dated as being 40,000 years old.[6]

Charles Choi in his article on the acquisition of clothing by humans[7] cites Doctor David Reed of the University of Florida who has studied lice in humans in order to understand human evolution and migration patterns. His study of the evolution of the clothes lice leads him to conclude that humans started to wear clothing 170,000 years ago. The presumption here is that clothing would be made from preserved animal skins.

Leather was clearly an important material for ancient man. When the discovery was made that water keeps fresh in a leather bag is not known but it must have been an important one allowing ancient tribes to wander further from water sources taking their water supply with them. Moulded raw-hides almost certainly preceded pottery for vessels.[8]

More recent evidence

There is clear evidence (including Otzi) of the use of leather from a variety of sources, and it has been used for bags, clothing, footwear, armour, tents and weapons, and in art for thousands of years. Leather sandals dating back more than 7,000 years have been discovered in caves in Missouri, although the wearing of shoes is thought to be much older than this (see 'Prehistoric', above).

An article by Kate Ravilious for the National Geographic Times[9] describes the find of the world's oldest leather shoe. In excellent condition, the so called Areni-1 shoe was found by a team led by archaeologist Boris Gasparyan in 2008 in a cave in Armenia close to the Iranian border. It was a size 4, (European size 37) which is a woman's size today but it may well have been worn by a man at that time. The shoe is made from a single piece of cured cowhide complete with laces. Radiocarbon dating revealed the shoe is 5,500 years old, making it slightly older than Otzi's. The fact that the shoe was preserved so well was put down to the cool dry conditions in the cave and that it was covered in a thick layer of sheep dung, which essentially preserved it over the millennia. The shoe is now on display at the History Museum of Armenia.

Photo 2.2; Allegedly the world's oldest shoe

Techniques of preserving animal skins developed independently throughout Asia, Europe and America. In primitive societies these techniques were often highly valued and passed down from father to son.

The early Egyptians were skilled in the use of leather using it for sandals, gloves, military equipment, weapons and liquid containers.

Evidence of leather trappings and harnesses used with chariots has been found in the tombs dating back 3,300 years. In an article 'World's First Prosthetic: Egyptian Mummy's Fake Toe' Charles Choi reports[10] on the find in 2000 of an artificial toe made from wood and leather found on the foot of an Egyptian mummy, (a woman estimated to be between 50-60 years old) in a tomb in Thebes. Based on other artifacts in the tomb, the wood and leather prosthesis is estimated to be from the period 1069 – 644 BC.

Photo 2.3; Prosthetic toe found on an Egyptian mummy

In Roman times leather was used for helmets and armour, shields, harnesses, clothing, footwear and even the sails of ships. Romans often wore sandals but more formal dress required that the *calceus* be worn – a shoe with slits at the sides and straps knotted at the front. Roman soldiers wore heavy duty leather sandals with straps wound around the lower leg; also often, a leather cap.

A leather tannery was discovered in the ruins of Pompeii which was covered in four to six metres of volcanic ash in AD 79. The Romans are thought to have brought leather making to Great Britain and a large number of leather items have been found while excavating Roman sites.

Leather was used in ancient Greece and is referred to in the works of Homer, dated somewhere between 750 and 650 BC.

Leather was used to make armour (amongst other things) throughout the Middle Ages, (5th to 15th centuries). Sometimes the leather was hardened with hot water, oil or wax, a process known as *Cuir Bouilli.*

The development of the leather-making process through the ages

The process of making leather changed little from Roman times until the late 19th to early 20th centuries which saw the introduction of chrome tanning, the use of tanning drums to replace vats and the development of the band splitter which can split leather into two or more layers. There were some innovations along the way however. Cordovan leather, originally produced in Spain, became famous throughout Europe from the 8th century. In Europe in the Middle Ages trade craftsmen united in trade guilds and this included tanners and leather workers and licences were issued to cover leather production. The use of lime as a means of accelerating the removal of animal hair from the hide was also discovered around this time.

The leather-making process

Leather making or tanning basically involves subjecting the rawhide or skin from an animal to a series of operations, both chemical and mechanical, with the aim of:

a. Isolating the base constituent of leather (the fibrous protein collagen) and removing all non-collagenous components.

b. Making the leather resistant to biological action – even when wet.
c. Imparting the desired physical and aesthetic characteristics, (softness, toughness, finish, etc.).

Our ancestors probably discovered the craft of leather making by accident

Skins obtained from animals as a result of hunting, and later farming, would have become stiff on drying, or if left in the wet state, putrefied. The earliest preservation methods probably involved rubbing skins with animal fats to make them more flexible and durable. A refinement on this would include smoking the skins by a fire, a process probably discovered by accident.

Medieval tanning methods

In medieval times the tanning operation was a grim business and for this reason tanneries were, (and still are) usually located on the edge of towns. Claire Burn's article 'The Tanning Industry of Medieval Britain'[11] provides a detailed picture of the tanning industry in Medieval times. Determinants of location included the availability of cattle and therefore hides, tanning materials including oak bark, and a water source such as a river or a stream. Tanning must have been an essential and relatively large-scale industry in medieval times as leather was in those days, as it is today, a popular and important material for apparel, footwear, upholstery, harnesses, saddles, and so on. Add to this the need for armour and vessels for holding liquids and one can imagine how important leather (and therefore the tanning industry) was prior to the emergence of modern day alternatives such as plastics, rubbers and synthetic fibres.

Photo 2.5; Fragments of leather shoes from the 14th or 15th century (alongside a replica of a complete boot), found in an area where tanneries were located outside the city walls of Chester, UK.

Animals, most often cattle hides, would arrive at the tannery from the abattoir, sometimes in a dried state and covered with blood, flesh, hair, fat and dung, and sometimes with the horns and hooves still attached. The hides were a by-product of butchery and the horns and hooves, having no real value, were often not removed. In fact the excavation of large numbers of horns and hooves provide a clue to the location of ancient tanning sites. Tanners had sole access to, and right to buy, hides.

Photo 2.4; A tannery in Marrakech, Morocco, which still today makes leather using ancient equipment and processes, producing items essentially for the tourist trade.

The first step would be to soak the skins in water to remove the gore and soften them, and prepare them for tanning. Any remaining fat and flesh would be removed by scraping. In order to remove the hair several methods were employed. The skins could be painted with an alkali lime paste; they could alternatively be soaked in urine. One technique was to sprinkle the hides with urine and store them in a warm environment, folded hair side in to encourage rotting of the hair follicles and thereby facilitating hair removal by scraping. The use of urine figures prominently in early tanning and 'piss pots' for the collection of urine (usually by

children), were a common site on street corners in towns located near tanneries.

Once the hair had been removed, tanners would 'bate' the skins which involved soaking them in a solution of warm water and dung, often dog dung as carnivore dung is particularly effective due to the presence of digestive enzymes. Pigeon or chicken dung was used subject to availability, and children were often employed as dung gathers. In bating, enzymes act to remove unwanted proteins and other constituents in the skin, to produce a softer, more pliable leather. The degree of bating depended on what the leather was to be used for. Glove leather needed to be soft so required a strong bate, soling leather less so.[12] A bating recipe from the time called for 14 quarts of dog dung for every four dozen skins, diluted to the consistency of honey.[13] The tanner would often use his feet to work the dung into the skins thigh deep in the mixture for several hours. Clearly this was an unpredictable process, not to say a highly unpleasant one. The first standardised bate enzymes obtained from slaughtered animals appeared in the early 1900s though bating using dog dung continued until the 1950s.[14] Bating is still a part of the modern leather-making process, but the enzymes used are now isolated from bacteria.

Bating is a process probably discovered by accident. Perhaps the observation was made that the area of leather made from a cow's rear which had been covered in dung was softer than from other parts of the animal?

The hides were then de-limed or 'drenched' using a variety of substances including barley or rye solutions, old beer and (again) more urine.

After these preparatory stages had been completed the actual tanning operation could be carried out. Tanning is a chemical treatment process whereby the perishable protein in an animal hide or skin, collagen, is converted into durable and flexible leather. At this stage the hide would be free of hair, fat, and other unwanted inter-fibrillary materials leaving an almost pure collagen fibre network. If the hide were to be dried at this stage it would form a stiff, hard material, largely unusable. To prevent this, a range of processes were carried out including mechanically 'working' the hide, stretching it to loosen it while drying, and introducing fats into the skin. A variety of materials were used for this purpose, including vegetable tanning agents, oils, alum, even animal brains. (The brain has a significant fat content and the size of a mammal's brain is just sufficient to tan its hide!)

Vegetable tanning

The technique known as vegetable tanning has been used for thousands of years. The earliest known leather tanning recipes date back 3,000 years to Babylonian times and include oil, fat, alum and gall nuts as tanning agents. The remains of mills used for crushing tree bark have been found dating back to these times. The bark of some trees, typically oak, and the leaves of several trees, nuts and plants contain a material called tannin which is particularly effective in preserving skins. (Early tanners were sometimes referred to as Barkers). We can imagine how this may have been discovered - perhaps animal skins may have been thrown over the bough of a tree in a wet state and left for some time and it was noticed that the skin was 'preserved' in the area where it came into contact with the tree. Or maybe the skin from an animal that had lain dead for a period of time in a pool containing a large amount of tannin-rich vegetable matter was found to have desirable properties. However it was discovered, vegetable tanning has been an effective means of preserving animal skins and converting them to leather throughout the ages.

The vegetable tanning operation involved placing the animal skins in shallow pits or vats filled with tannin solution, usually made by ground-up tree bark such as oak in water. More bark was added periodically and the skins left until the tannin solution had penetrated all the way through the skin structure – a process that could take several months, even a year or more depending on the thickness of the hide and the purpose for which it was intended. Claire Burns cites the oath of the Leicester tanners which required well-tanned leather to be soaked in tanning solution for 'a year and a day' before being sold[11]. (Modern vegetable tanned leather takes just a few weeks to manufacture using drums).

Hides would then be rinsed, smoothed and dried under controlled conditions, perhaps in a dark shed, prior to stretching, shaving and the application of tallow, oils and greases to promote suppleness. The finished leather would then be sold on to leather craftsmen.

Photo 2.6; A modern vegetable tanned leather briefcase

The vegetable tanning process continues to be used commercially to this day with about 10 per cent of all leather produced being manufactured using this method. Vegetable tanned leathers tend to be rather stiff and firm; ideal for shoe soles, luggage, equine leathers, etc. However, there are several techniques available to make vegetable tanned leather softer such as dry milling; see the chapter 5, Leather Finishes.

Parchment and vellum

No discussion of ancient skin and hide treatment would be complete without mentioning parchment and vellum.

Leather, despite its strength and toughness, is not suitable for the long-term preservation of written documents. As leather ages over long periods of time it loses its natural oils and becomes brittle, eventually breaking down to dust. Some ancient documents made from leather still do survive though, but one of the reasons cited for the preservation of the Dead Sea Scrolls that predate Christ is that most of them were written on vellum and parchment which does not involve tanning materials in its production.

Parchment, which has been used since at least the sixth century BC, is produced by washing the animal's skin and treating it with lime, an inorganic material containing calcium. The skin was then dried under tension and abraded with pumice stone to produce a smooth surface. The resulting parchment was strong, and could be written upon on both sides. The finest parchment was called vellum and was made from the skin of calves or goats (kids), with that from newly or still born animals being particularly highly prized.

Interestingly, scholars believe that there may be a hierarchy in the religious importance of the Dead Sea Scrolls, the most religiously significant

Photo 2.7; A section of one of the Dead Sea Scrolls

being written on goat and calf skins and the less significant being written on the skins of gazelle and ibex.

Modern methods of leather making

According to leather historian and author John Waterer "The tanning and dressing of leather was one of the last occupations to leave the middle ages behind".[15] However there have been significant changes to the tanning process following the industrial revolution.

In the 19th century the improvement in transportation links allowed for the import of improved vegetable tanning agents such as Quebracho bark from South America and Mimosa bark from Australia. These eventually became exported as dried liquid extracts which aided transportation and improved concentration, effectiveness and consistency; this has allowed tanning times to be reduced from several months to a few weeks. These materials are still in use today.

Chrome tanning discovered

The discovery of chrome as a tanning agent in the late 19th century revolutionised the leather tanning industry. By the 1840s medical practitioners were using sutures made from animal skin stabilised by soaking in a chrome solution; it was found that the sutures could be made softer and more pliable by treating them with glycerol, [16] . The further development of this discovery was triggered by an interesting problem. The white, alum tanned leather used to cover ladies' corset stays turned brown with use. The problem was given to American chemist Augustus Schultz. In his search for a leather type that would stay permanently white he found that chromium salts produced a new type of leather and he patented the process in 1884. The first

leathers produced in this way were hard stiff and blue, very different to vegetable tanned leathers produced at the time; however the tanning time was much reduced and this prompted others to perfect the process. A tanner, Robert Foerderer learned how to treat chrome-tanned leather with soaps and oils to make it soft and pliable, (a process known today as 'fat-liquoring'). Chrome-tanned leather eventually replaced the heavier bark-tanned leather previously used to make shoe uppers.

The American Henry Proctor, author of 'The Textbook of Tanning'[17] in 1885 is credited with the introduction of chrome tanning into Europe in around 1895. This was an important innovation allowing leather with a whole range of interesting new properties to be produced in a matter of days rather than months. At around the same time, tanning pits began to be substituted by rotating drums. Today something approaching 85% of leathers are 'chrome' tanned.

Another import from America in the late 19th century was the band knife splitting machine. This allowed cow hides, which could be 5-10 millimetres thick, to be fed into one end of the machine and emerge at the other end accurately split into two or more layers to give 'grain splits' (the outer or hair side of the hide) and 'flesh

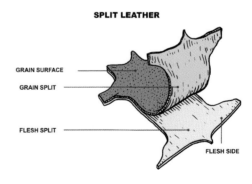

How a skin can be split into layers

Photo 2.7; Ecco Shoes' modern tannery in Dongen, Holland

splits' (the inner side of the hide) – more about these later. Prior to the introduction of the splitting machine, the only way of obtaining thin leather other than laborious and difficult hand slicing was to use naturally thin leather such as sheep, goat or calf.

The two World Wars in the 20th century resulted in a shortage of vegetable tanning agents and this encouraged the development of synthetic synthetic materials, now known as syntans, which are also still used today to make leather with some interesting properties. Several other tanning agents have also been developed and these will be reviewed later.

Since the middle of the last century, and in order to meet the demand for more attractive and fashionable leather, great inroads have been made in terms of leather finishing techniques. Finishes comprise of a wide variety of coloured pigments, binders, oils and waxes, films etc. that are applied to the surface of leather to improve performance and/or for fashion or aesthetic reasons. Now leather can be finished in a huge range of shades and colours. It can be embossed to produce fake animal prints and laminated with films to produce a range of interesting leather types including patent leather. It can be sprayed with oil and wax to produce attractive pull-up leathers or buffed to make nubucks and suedes.

Increasing waste disposal costs, European Union and other legislation, and rising environmental awareness generally, has put the focus on more environmentally friendly tanning methods over the past 15-20 years. Now tanners and chemical suppliers are constantly seeking new ways to reduce and recycle waste and chemicals, and minimise water and energy costs. In some cases chemicals are replaced altogether in particular processes by using enzymes which are proteins (mostly) that catalyse chemical reactions and processes in leather making such as soaking, dehairing and bating.

The modern tanning operation sees raw hides passing through a range of processes requiring careful control of time, temperature, acidity (pH), mechanical action and chemical dosages. Automation of many processes has served to improve consistency and now chrome leather can be made in two to three days. Vegetable tanned leather using exotic tanning agents, enzymes and tanning in revolving drums rather than pits can be produced in a few weeks rather than several months.

The modern tanning operation will be discussed in detail in chapter 6.

Chapter 2 References:

1. Jablonski, N. (2004). *The Evolution of Human Skin and Skin Colour*. Annu. Rev. Anthropol. 2004. 33:585-623.

2. Thompson, R. S. (1997). *When did chrome tanning start?* Leather Conservation News 13.1.

3. Tanners Council of America. (1937). *The Romance of Leather and its Importance to Mankind*. American Leather Producers, New York.

4. Pickrell, J. (October 2005). [On-line]. *Toe Bones Reveal World's Earliest Shoe Wearers*. [National Geographic]. Available from http://news.nationalgeographic.com. Accessed: 13/12/2013.

5. Becky Wragg Sykes. (20/05/2013). [On-line].*Who invented Clothes? A Paleolithic Archaeologist Answers.* Available at www.theguardian.com. Accessed 09/11/2014.

6. Calloway, E. (2013). [On-line]. *Neanderthals make leather-working tools like those in use today.* Nature, (12 August 2013). Available at: www.nature.com. Accessed: 4/4/2015.

7. Choi, C Q. (07/01/2011). [On-line]. *Humans got lice when we clothed our naked, hairless bodies.* Available at www.lifescience.com. Accessed: 16/07/2014.

8. Forbes, RJ, (1996). *Studies in Ancient Technology*, Bind 6. E J Brill, Liden, Netherlands.

9. Ravilious, K. (June 2010). [On-line]. *World's Oldest Leather Shoe Found – Stunningly Preserved.* National Geographic. Available from http://news.nationalgeographic.com. Accessed: 12/12/2013.

10. Choi, C. (27/07/2007). [On-line] *World's First Prosthetic: Egyptian Mummy's Fake Toe.* Available at: www.lifescience.com. Accessed 08/12/2014.

11. Burns, C. (15/06/2012). *The Tanning Industry of Medieval Britain*. [On-line]. Available at http://antrojournal.com. Accessed 11/06/2014.

12. Straathof & Aldercreutz, (2005). *Applied Biocatalysis*. CRC Press, second edition.

13. Kanigel, R. (2007). *Faux Real: Genuine Leather and 200 Years of Inspired Fakes.* Joseph Henry Press.

14. Redwood, M (n.d). [on-line] Blog, www.mikeredwood.com. Accessed 22/07/2015.

15. Waterer, J W. (1950). *Leather and Craftsmanship*. Faber.

16. Lampard, G. (2013). [On-line]. *A History of New Ideas in Tanning*. Leather International. Available at www.leathermag.com. Accessed on 11/03/2015.

17. Proctor, H R. (1885). *A Text Book of Tanning: A Treatise on the Conversion of Skins into Leather, both Practical and Theoretical*. E & F N Spon. London & New York.

Chapter 2 Photographs:

2.1. By kind permission of The South Tyrol Museum of Archeaology

2.2 & 2.3. Wikipedia.org

2.4. M G Mirams & P J McElheron

2.5. M G Mirams & P J McElerhon, by kind permission Sole Trader of Chester and acknowledgement to the Chester Grosvenor Museum

2.6. Zebrik, Dreamstime.com

2.7. Byjeng, Dreamstime.com

2.8. M G Mirams & P J McElheron, by kind permission of Ecco Shoes A/S

CHAPTER 3, TYPES OF LEATHER

So far we have talked generically about 'leather' as being a material from which clothing, footwear, furniture and other items have been made throughout the centuries. Leather can be made from hides and skins from a large range of creatures: mammals, birds, reptiles and even fish, and manufactured and finished in so many ways that we now need to start thinking about the variety of leather types (the most common in this chapter and the more exotic in chapter 4) and the range of finishes (chapter 5), each of which gives the material specific characteristics and qualities that make it more or less suitable for the variety of products and applications for which it is used.

The Structure of Leather

Hides and Skins: The term 'hide' generally refers to the outer covering of large animals such as cows, water buffalo etc, whereas 'skin' is used for smaller animals like sheep, goats and pigs, as well as the immature animals of the larger species (such as calves and colts). The term 'skin' is also used for reptiles, birds and fishes.

To be able to differentiate between the main leather types and understand their properties, we need to know something about the structure of leather.

Fresh skins and hides removed from the animal consist of a lot of water (over 60 percent), proteins, fatty material and some mineral salts. The actual composition of a raw hide, taken directly from the animal, consists mainly of collagen and water.

The most important constituent from a leather perspective is the collagen which is a fibrous protein, insoluble in water and it is this element in the animal's skin that ultimately becomes leather. It is all that is remaining from the original animal skin in finished leather, the other materials, including much of the water, having been removed in the tanning process. A fresh animal skin contains around 33 percent protein

of which about 29 percent is collagen. It is important to remove the other non-structural proteins during tanning. In living skin they provide key functions such as promoting growth; however when the skin is dried, they dry to a hard glue-like material which serves to cement the collagen fibres together making the resultant leather hard and stiff.

Finished leather is essentially made up of numerous fibre bundles of collagen. These bundles are closely interwoven to form a strong, tough, flexible, permeable structure. All mammalian skin follows the same basic structure but varies greatly in shape, size and thickness.

Variations in structure

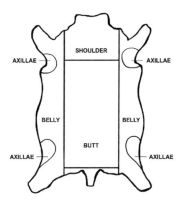

A typical animal hide, showing the various regions

The collagen structures, and therefore the properties of leather, vary within the hide or skin. The skin in the neck and shoulder region tends to be thicker than the rest of the skin in order to give the animal greater protection from predators in the wild. A series of wrinkles are also a feature of the neck region resulting from the constant bending of the neck as the animal feeds. The belly region is thin and stretchy relative to the other part of the hide; the collagen fibres are less compact here allowing them to stretch. This is because, in life, this region of the hide has to stretch easily as the animal feeds, or while bearing young. This has consequences for finished leather goods; leather from the belly regions is not suitable for furniture seat panels which would remain in a semi stretched state and appear baggy after continued use. Such may be fine for non-stressed regions of furniture like the rear or side panels. The same principle applies for elbow and knee regions in leather garments. At the four corners of the belly the axillae are situated where the limbs join the body; these regions have to be very flexible to facilitate walking and running but leather made from these regions is very thin, stretchy and unsightly with potentially many deep wrinkles and creases. It is only suitable for non-visible areas such as the tongue in footwear.

The area referred to as the butt has the most uniform and compact structure and is the prime cutting area for most leather goods as it is the strongest and most durable region of the hide. It is the area which is consistently the most aesthetically pleasing, and stands up well to general wear and tear.

Leather utilisation is a major concern of anyone who uses leather commercially. The cost of the leather represents a major proportion of the finished cost of the article being manufactured be that a shoe, a jacket or a sofa. Ideally every square centimetre should be used and, taking a shoe as an example, this means that the most visible part of the shoe, the vamp or forepart, will be cut from the butt region, the counters or sidepieces may be cut from the shoulder and the tongue, which is largely hidden, can be cut from the belly region. The same principle also applies to other leather goods.

Another point we need to address here is 'lines of tightness'. The fibre structures in leather are not randomly orientated, rather they follow the direction of hair growth. Leather exhibits a higher degree of stretch if it is pulled in the same direction as the collagen fibres are oriented. Leather is termed 'tight', or less stretchy in the direction indicated, see the diagram. This is an important consideration when cutting components for clothing and footwear. For example leather components for shoes need to be 'tight' in the heel to toe direction and so components must be cut accordingly.

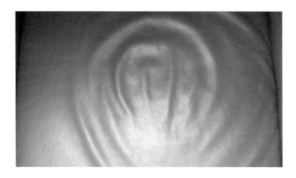

Photo 3.1; A 'baggy' sofa seat, caused by using leather that is too stretchy, probably from the belly region of a cow hide

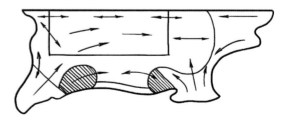

Lines of tightness

Variations in grain surface and structure between species

We shall use the structure of cow leather as our starting point and later compare this with calf skin, sheep, goat and pig skin.

Cattle (bovine) leather

The large production of cattle hides in the United States and Europe is a significant factor in the supply of leather. A high standard of living and a taste for beef means plenty is available. Dairy cattle are raised for their production of milk and a dairy cow will produce between 25 and 40 litres of milk per day, depending on the breed and other factors. When it is no longer able to deliver this amount, it is slaughtered. The hide tends to be thinner, more stretchy and with a lower fat content than that of beef cattle. The younger the animal - the thinner the leather and the finer the grain. Younger skins tend to be relatively free from insect damage, scratches and other related features.

The 'grain' layer has a relatively smooth surface that would have been covered in hair before being removed in the tanning process. Cow leather has a distinctive grain pattern. The grain surface is the grain layer visible when the

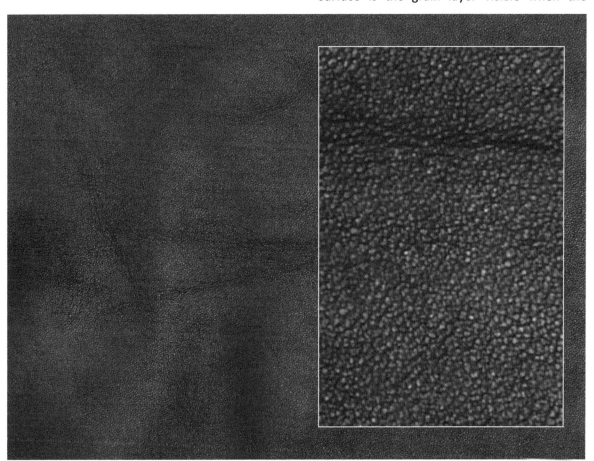

Photo 3.2; The surface of cow leather

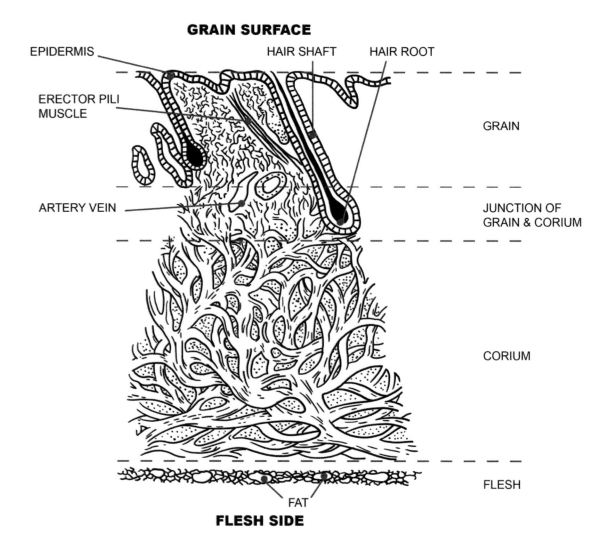

GRAIN SURFACE

EPIDERMIS

ERECTOR PILI MUSCLE

ARTERY VEIN

HAIR SHAFT   HAIR ROOT

GRAIN

JUNCTION OF GRAIN & CORIUM

CORIUM

FLESH

FAT

FLESH SIDE

A cross-section of cow leather

epidermis is removed in tanning; when viewed under a magnifying glass (X10), the pattern of hair follicles can be easily seen. The hair follicles are of uniform size, packed closely together and give a distinctive grain pattern which can be used to distinguish the species from which the leather was made.

The surface appearance of the leather will depend on many factors such as sex, breed and the health and nutrition of the animal.

When un-split bovine leather is viewed in cross-section, the fibrous structure of the leather is easily seen. The thickness of cow hide is typically around 5 to 10 millimetres, this can vary considerably depending on breed, sex and age of the animal. This is too thick for practically all purposes, footwear for example uses leather that is 1.2 - 1.4 millimetres for everyday footwear and up to 2 millimetres or more for boots. Leather is therefore usually split into two or

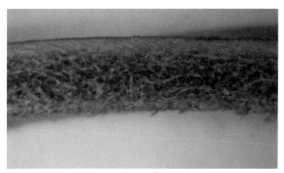

Photo 3.3; Cross-section of cow leather

more layers, (more about this later). The grain layer makes up approximately one fifth of the total thickness of the cattle hide and this ratio – one fifth grain to four fifths corium, (corium is Latin for leather), remains constant regardless of the overall hide thickness. The grain layer is weak relative to the corium. Tests have revealed that the grain layer in bovine leathers has only 20 percent the tear strength of the corium layer, so, if thin leather is required, it is important to ensure that the split contains sufficient corium leather to retain strength. An option is to use hides with a thin grain layer, for example cow (female) hides which are thinner than steer (male) hides. Calf skin would also be a possibility but this is relatively expensive.

The corium contains larger fibre bundles. The distinction between the grain and the corium is an important one. In the grain layer, the collagen fibres are finer than those in the corium and tightly interwoven, so much so that there are no loose ends at the surface. When the protective layer of keratinous cells called the epidermis is removed in the tanning process, the grain surface, characteristic of the animal type, remains.

The junction is the area between the grain and the corium. In cattle the grain and corium are well intermingled and the transition from grain to corium is gradual. In the corium, the collagen fibres are also tightly interwoven at various angles but the fibres are courser and stronger, which makes the corium the strongest part of the leather. The angle of the fibres has an effect on leather properties. Upright, tightly woven fibres result in a firmer leather with little stretch. Horizontal, loosely woven fibres will result in a softer leather with more stretch.

Cow leather is used for a wide range of applications including footwear, apparel, upholstery, auto leathers, gloves and accessories.

Calfskin

Calfskins are a by-product of the dairy industry, (and the veal industry in Europe) and are therefore available in all dairy producing areas of the world. Calves are slaughtered a few weeks after birth and so the grain surface of calf leather has a fine, tight grain structure free from damage, scratches, insect bites, etc. relative to an older animal. The skin has a high value due to its fine, tight grain structure and freedom from defects. The collagen fibre bundles are much smaller than adult cattle hides.

Calf skin is thin, often just over a millimetre, so it is ideal for applications requiring thin leather but it is expensive and has a limited cutting area due to its small size.

Domestic sheep (ovine) leather

There are many different types of breeds of sheep available from many parts of the world and with quite widely differing characteristics. Their skins vary greatly in size, as does the amount of wool, which generally has a higher value than the skin and can weigh twice as much.

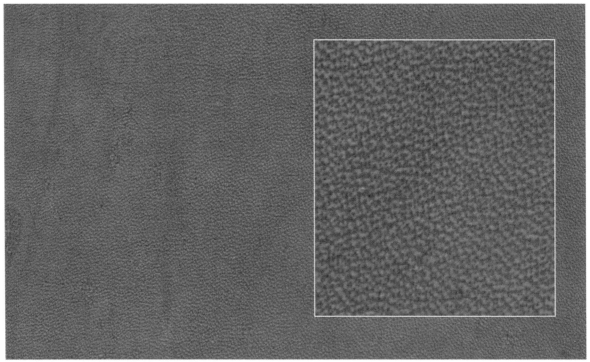

Photo 3.4; The surface of calf leather

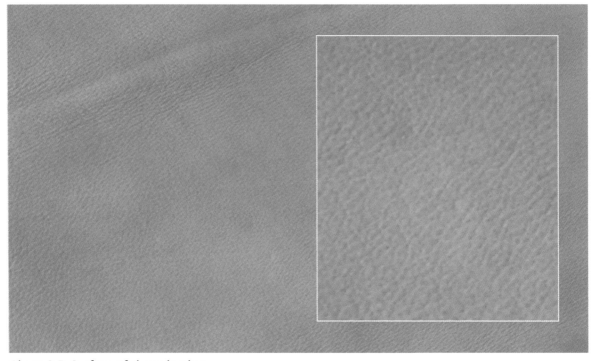

Photo 3.5; Surface of sheep leather

The surface of sheep leather

Sheep skins can be processed retaining the wool. However, for most applications the wool is removed in the tannery. Sheep have been selectively bred over centuries to produce large amounts of wool and this is apparent when looking at the grain surface of sheep leather. There are many more hair follicles relative to cow leather. These are arranged in groups with spaces in between. These spaces allow the tanner to give the leather a 'polish' resulting in a pleasant glossy appearance which many find appealing and without loss of the leather's natural 'feel'.

When viewed in cross section, the collagen fibre structure of sheepskin differs considerably from cattle leather.

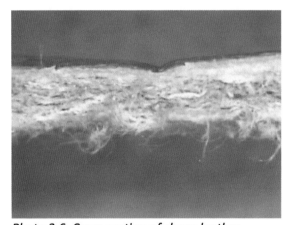

Photo 3.6; Cross-section of sheep leather

Sheep are much smaller than cows so the skin is obviously smaller, typically 3-14 square feet compared to 40-plus square feet for a cow. The skin is thinner, usually 0.7-0.9 millimetres so it is not necessary to split sheep leather. The collagen fibre bundles are much finer and, if the flesh side of sheep skin is lightly buffed, this produces a fine suede leather, much finer than a cow suede.

Whilst most of the world has adopted the metric system for measurements, the area measurement of leather is still made using the 'imperial' units of square feet. Therefore we frequently get the seemingly conflicting units of measurement between leather thickness or 'substance' is given millimetres whilst the hide or skin area is stated in square feet!

The ratio of the thickness of grain to corium is also very different in sheep skin; the grain layer makes up almost half of the thickness, (compared to 20 percent with cow hide). Also the transition from grain to corium is very distinct, unlike in cattle hides where it is gradual. Indeed, a potential problem with sheep skin is the grain and the corium separating during tanning or in use; this is referred to as 'looseness' and manifests itself as wrinkles in the finished leather. The reason for this is that sheep are relatively fatty animals, with fat making up around 25 percent of the skin. A layer of fat cells is deposited between the grain and corium and the removal of this fat during the tanning process can cause the two layers to separate, particularly when repeatedly flexed. The lesser the amount of hair or wool on an animal, the stronger the resultant leather - there are fewer 'holes' in the grain layer. Sheep have a lot of wool (or hair in some species) which weakens the grain layer significantly, resulting in a low tear strength relative to other leather types.

Sheep skin is very soft with a very good 'drape' and is used for clothing, gloves, hats, indoor footwear, rugs and pelts.

Goat or kid (caprine) leather

Goats are tough animals that can exist on a wide variety of foods. They supply meat, milk and, naturally, leather. The quality of goat leather can vary considerably depending on the source and

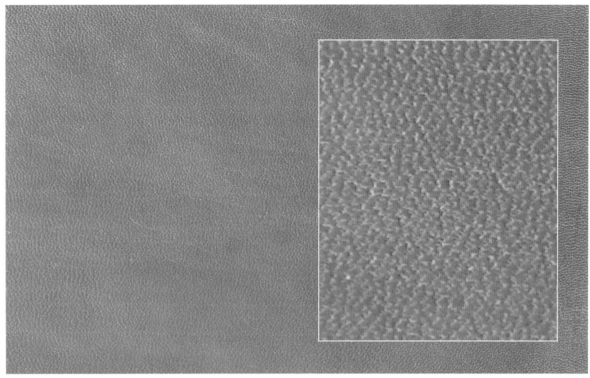

Photo 3.7; Surface of goat leather

how the animals have been raised. Although goat and sheep skins are similar in size and thickness, there are some significant differences when it comes to their leather.

Goats are not raised to produce wool and the density of the hair follicles is similar to that of cattle. For most species there are two sizes of hair; fine undercoat and longer, stiffer 'guard hairs'. When these have been removed in the tannery, the two types of hair follicles remain. They are arranged in lines or tracks of large ones from the guard hairs closely followed by a line of small ones, from the undercoat.

The grain pattern on goat leather can vary in evenness of grain size and the presence of wrinkles, and can be less attractive than other leather types. However, the fine collagen fibre structure means that the backside (flesh side) of

the leather can be buffed to produce very fine, attractive suede.

In cross section, the thickness of the grain layer relative to the corium is less than that of sheep skin but is greater than that of cattle skin.

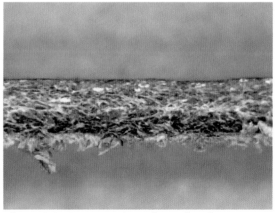

Photo 3.8; Cross-section of goat leather

Goatskin has much less hair than sheep and so the grain layer is not weakened to the same extent as sheep skin. As with cattle skin, there is a gradual transition between grain and corium as goats do not have a layer of fat in between the grain and corium. As a result, goatskin is not prone to looseness and makes a lightweight leather, with thickness in the range 0.7 – 0.9 millimetres, resistant to flexing and with high strength. This allows it to be used in a wide range of applications including ladies footwear, apparel, gloves and small furniture items. Untanned goat skin can be used for parchment and drum heads.

Pigskin (porcine) leather

Pigskin accounts for about 10 percent of all leather made, although often the skin is left on the carcase after slaughter or used for the production of gelatine. Most of the world's pigskin is of Chinese origin.

The surface of pig skin.

Pig skin leather is perhaps the easiest to identify. The surface of pig leather when viewed under a magnifying glass has a rough, almost nodular appearance. Pigs have relatively few hairs (or bristles) and the hair follicle pattern reflects this. The follicles are arranged in a trio, triangular pattern in many species, (which, incidentally, means that it is easily reproduced in printed imitations). Pigs can be quite aggressive animals and the way they are raised and their lack of protective hair can result in damage to the grain surface of the leather. This is one of the reasons why pig leather is often made as a suede. When

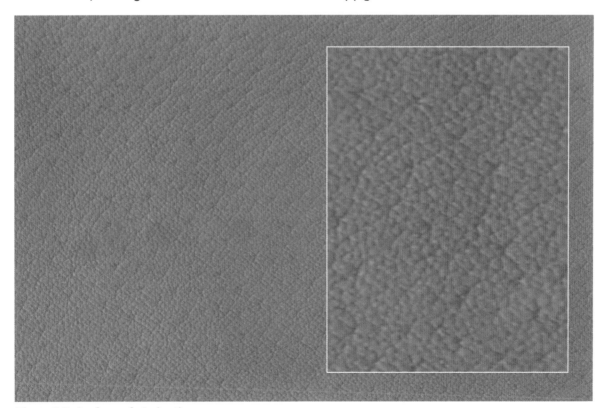

Photo 3.9; Surface of pig leather

making a suede, if the surface buffing is not done carefully, the difference in the collagen fibre structure surrounding the hair follicles results in a 'fisheye' effect surrounding each follicle, which can be unsightly.

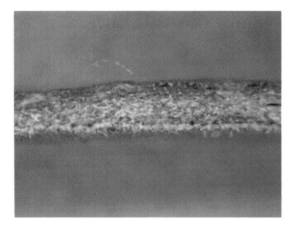

Photo 3.10; Cross-section of pig leather

The structure of pigskin is really very different from cow, sheep and goat skins. First of all, in cross section, the hair follicles are not confined to the grain layer but penetrate the full skin thickness, from one side to the other. Actually pig skin is all grain layer, there is no difference between the grain layer and the corium. This does not mean pigskin leather is weak, quite the reverse. Pigs skin has few hair follicles allowing space for collagen fibre bundles which impart strength, also the collagen fibre bundles are finel and compact. This results in a compact structure allowing the leather to be split thinly without significant loss of strength.

As the hair follicles penetrate all the way through the leather from grain to flesh side, it is said to be difficult to make pig leather waterproof.

Pig skin is useful when a strong, yet thin leather is required, for example for hardwearing shoe linings, saddlery, and gloves. In thicker form it is suitable for clothing and suede shoes. It does have less drape than sheepskin, tending to form stiff 'folds'; however pig suede is softer and frequently used for apparel.

Chapter 3 References:

We have used material from a number of sources to support the narrative in this chapter, and acknowledge the following:

All-about-leather. [On-line]. *Leather Types*. Available at www.all-about-leather.co.uk.

International Council of Tanners. [On-line]. *Introduction to Leather*. Avalaible at www.leathercouncil.org.

Leathernet. [On-line]. *Leather Types – Process Production and Forms of Leather*. Available at www.leathernet.com/leather.htm.

Michel, A. (2014) *Skin Deep: An Outline of the Structure of Different Skins and how it Influences Behaviour in Use*. In: Harris, S & Veldmeijer, A J (eds.). Ehy Leather: The Material and Cultural Dimensions of Leather. Sidestone Press.

Mwingihija, M. (2014). [On-line*]. Emerging World Leather Trends and Continental Shifts on Leather and Leather Goods Production*. Available at www.scribesguildjournals.org.

Sharphouse, J H. (1983). *Leather Technicians Handbook*. Leather Producers' Association.

Sorensen Leather. [On-line*]. Comparison of Aniline, Semi-aniline and Pigmented Leather by Sorensen Leather* (video). Available at https://Youtube.com.

Chapter 3 Photographs:

All photographs in this chapter: M G Mirams & P J McElheron.

CHAPTER 4, MORE EXOTIC TYPES OF LEATHER

The skins from virtually all vertebrate animals can be, and are, made into leather - the basic rule is that if you can skin it, you can make leather from it. In this chapter we will review the main types of leather that fall into the category of 'exotic leathers'.

CITES (the Convention on International Trade in Endangered Species of Wild Fauna and Flora) is a legally binding international agreement between governments. Its aim is to ensure that international trade in specimens of wild animals and plants does not threaten their survival. CITES currently has 180 members. Endangered species are listed in three appendices depending on the level of protection assessed as being needed. For more information visit www.cities.org.

Appendix I includes species threatened with extinction. Trade in specimens of these species is permitted only in exceptional circumstances.

Appendix II includes species not necessarily threatened with extinction, but in which trade must be controlled in order to avoid utilisation incompatible with their survival.

Appendix III contains species that are protected in at least one country, which has asked other CITES Parties for assistance in controlling the trade.

A specimen of a CITES-listed species may be imported into or exported (or re-exported) from a State party to the Convention only if the appropriate documentation has been obtained and presented for clearance at the port of entry or exit. There is some variation of the requirements from one country to another and it is always necessary to check on the national laws that may be stricter, (CITES.org).

Horse leather

Not exotic exactly, but perhaps a little unusual. In addition to being companion animals and pets, horses are sport and working animals. Relative to cattle, horses are poor converters of grass and grain to meat so tend not to be bred and raised in the UK or USA specifically for their meat. Here, they are usually slaughtered when their commercial value, or their use as work animals (or sporting value in the case of race horses), no longer covers the cost of their upkeep.

According to an article by Jamie Doward in 2010, in the UK around 8,000 horses and ponies are slaughtered for their meat each year, half of which being thorougbreds.[1] The meat is exported, and the skin is a by-product. Horses are however slaughtered for meat in Asia and South America, and in several European countries, principally Italy, France, Spain, Belgium, Germany and the Netherlands.

Leather from horses is used for high-end products by the fashion and footwear industries. The leather is soft, supple and durable with an attractive, light grain structure. When vegetable tanned it is used for luggage, furniture, belts and equine leathers. When chrome tanned it is used for bags, footwear, gloves, etc. The main problem is consistency. Whereas cattle are slaughtered for human consumption and are

It's a common misconception that horse meat is a constituent in pet food. This was the case in the 1920s; according to Nestle, slaughterhouses opened pet food companies to dispose of horse meat. [2] This practice was phased out in the 1950s and most pet food companies would deny using horse meat.They would be required to list it as an ingredient on the label and, it is thought, this may discourage people purchasing the product.

uniform in terms of age and size, this is not generally true for horses which come in a wide variety of shapes and sizes. The most consistent supplies come from France, Belgium, Scandinavia, the UK and the USA. Supplies are increasing from China.

Special mention should be made of Shell Cordovan leather which is made from the rump area of the horse hide where the skin is thickest and toughest. The shells or ovals are actually made from the flat fibrous muscle from this region and are usually vegetable tanned – it's a lengthy process that may take six months but the result is a smooth, pliable, high quality product that could last a lifetime. It is used for footwear where it is resistant to the frequent creasing that often results between the toe box and the laces with other leather types. Cordovan is used for

Photo 4.1; Cordovan leather boots

wallets and a few specialised applications, for example for finger protection for archers. Demand exceeds supply and this is reflected in the high price for this leather type.

The consumption of horse meat is largely taboo in several countries in the western world, notably the UK and America. This is due to the horse's place in the culture as a pet or companion, for religious reasons, or their status as working and sporting animals.

Several animal welfare organisations such as World Horse Welfare and the Humane Society have criticised the poor conditions that over 65,000 horses per year have to endure in transport, which may take several days in cramped conditions. [3] The Humane Society also highlights the problems occurring with the slaughter of horses. They are flight animals, unlike cattle and have an instinctive desire to escape the abatoir making them difficult to stun prior to slaughter. [4]

Kangaroo leather

Kangaroos, which are native to Australia, are not farmed. They live in free-roaming herds and are hunted in the wild. They are protected by law but can be culled by licensed hunters. They are regarded by many in Australia as pests as they allegedly damage crops and knock down fences. The numbers of kangaroos can vary widely and when the population increases beyond a certain point in a particular area, they are culled and the meat and the hides sold (3.7 million animals in 2008). Six million

kangaroos were earmarked for slaughter in 2013.

Firstly, let's deal with the properties of the leather. The collagen fibre bundles in kangaroo leather have a highly uniform orientation parallel to the skin surface. Compare this to the collagen fibres in cattle leather that are almost in a random orientation. This structural uniformity and lack of fat cells in kangaroo leather explains the greater tensile strength of the material. Also it means that the leather can be split thinly and still retain its strength. When split to thin layers or substances, kangaroo leather retains much more of its original tensile strength relative to cattle leather. For example, measurements carried out in the VIA University College laboratory in Denmark indicate that, when split to 20 percent of its original thickness, kangaroo leather retains about half of its original tensile strength. Cow leather similarly split to 20 percent of its original thickness retains only 5 - 15 percent of its original strength. This opens some interesting possibilities as thinner means lighter weight. Examples where this is useful and where

Photo 4.2; Hats made from kangaroo leather

kangaroo leathers are used include motorcycle leathers and sports footwear.

However, there are some animal welfare issues concerning kangaroos which have resulted in a consumer backlash and several brands dropping products made with kangaroo leather. Although the culling practice is highly regulated to ensure it is both sustainable and humane, it has attracted much criticism from animal welfare activists. Problems include 'scattershot' resulting in animals not being killed cleanly and the treatment of baby kangaroos called 'joeys', many of which are left to die when the mother is shot, (the Australian government guidelines insist on the clubbing or decapitation of joeys).

Some question what they claim are myths and misinformation surrounding the slaughter of kangaroos. A report by zoologist and founder-director of Vival, Juliet Gellatley entitled 'Killing for Kicks' claims that kangaroos do not in fact compete with other farm animals and cites several credible studies confirming that kangaroos were not keen on farm crops and do not compete with sheep for food. [5] Also kangaroos are largely culled in areas that produce little in the way of crops and meat. Still others state that assigning kangaroos pest status contributes to the justification for the lack of humane treatment in their slaughter.

The majority of kangaroo meat is exported to countries including Russia and several European countries, principally France and Germany. China is seen as a market with great potential. Attempts by several market leading supermarkets to sell kangaroo meat in the UK in the period 1997-2000 were halted due to complaints from animal rights groups. Some kangaroo meat is used in pet food.

There are several petitions on the internet calling users of Kangaroo leather to cease the practice.

In 2006, the England footballer David Beckham switched from kangaroo leather football boots to synthetic materials after been made aware, by an animal rights group, of the cruelty involved in the slaughter of kangaroos.

The sporting brand Adidas agreed to discontinue the use of kangaroo leather in their prestige football boots in 2012 following complaints of animal cruelty. According to an article by Sean Poulter in the Daily Mail, Adidas plans to reduce its use of kangaroo leather in other products by 98 percent within 12 months. [6] Other brands also appear to be cutting the use of kangaroo leather following pressure from animal rights groups.

The Australian kangaroo industry would maintain that culls are highly regulated and controlled by government management plans and of the 48 species of kangaroo, only five are commonly harvested under strict supervision. The export of live animals is not permitted. Some experts are of the opinion that the controlled culling of kangaroos is a more environmentally friendly livestock option than the introduction of cattle and sheep.

Deer skin

Deerskin leather was used by Native American Indians to make clothing, footwear (moccasins), and a wide range of accessories. The colonists soon learned the advantages with deerskin, also adopting it for many of applications. Today, the majority of deer leather comes from farmed animals.

Photo 4.3; Camel leather items for sale in a tourist market in Marrakech

Deerskin is a very soft and supple leather, tough, almost with a spongy texture, very comfortable to wear and different from cow leather in several respects. It is not as hard wearing but is so elastic that it can stretch excessively in wear, (in fact some manufacturers 'pre-stretch' the leather prior to assembly).

Deer skin is used for apparel, footwear and high quality accessories, gloves and wallets. It commands a high price due to its relative rarity.

Camel leather

Camels are important animals in the Middle East providing transport, milk, meat and leather. Camel leather has a high collagen fibre density relative to bovine leather in order to provide the animal with adequate protection in the harsh environment in which it lives, this contributes to a tough, durable, yet supple leather.

The camel's shape, small body and long legs, (relative to bovine animals) is a challenge for furniture makers but the leather is used for footwear, bags and tourist items.

The leather is available with hair on, or with a smooth, suede or nubuck finish.

Ostrich leather

Ostriches are farmed for their meat, feathers and skin, and the hide has considerable value, higher than that of the the meat in most regions including Europe. For many people, ostrich leather is regarded as the most luxurious In the world with its distinctive pattern created by the quill marks differentiating it from other leather types. The skin has a high natural oil content making the leather soft, supple and resistant to cracking, and yet strong and durable.

Ostriches were first farmed in the 1850s, primarily for their feathers which were used to make ladies' hats - horse drawn carriages had made flamboyant hats very fashionable. Mass production of the automobile, which made wearing such hats impractical, virtually put an end to this fashion and the ostrich farming industry went quiet for the next 50 years until demand for ostrich meat began to increase. The marketing of ostrich leather began in the late 1960s and became popular in high fashion and for cowboy boots. Even the skin from the ostrich legs is used. Since then ostrich farming has spread to many countries where ostriches have been described as relatively easy to farm, although they can be dangerous and need to be managed carefully.

Ostrich leather is very distinctive with raised bumps which are the quill follicles, the most desirable feature of the leather, most

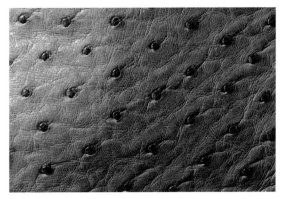

Photo 4.4; Surface of ostrich leather showing the distinctive quill marks

pronounced at the crown which is the back of the bird. Only about a third of the skin has these skin bumps, the sides of the skin are relatively smooth and it is the so-called 'full quill' products that demand the highest price.

The highest quality leather is free from holes or scratches. It should not be possible to see through the quill points if you hold the leather up to the light as this would indicate excessive shaving or poor handling in the tannery. The leather is soft but very strong; quill points should be firm and the leather should have a consistent colour.

Photo 4.5; Hat made from ostrich leather

Ostrich leather is usually coloured with transparent dyes and sprayed with a wax finish to provide some protection yet ensure the surface grain remains visible.

Fashion drives demand and many designer ranges have ostrich products such as handbags, wallets, shoes or boots. The automobile industry also uses ostrich leather for seats and door panels.

There are some animal welfare issues surrounding the farming and slaughter of ostriches, particularly in Europe. The UK based animal welfare organization, the Royal Society for the

Protection of Animals (RSPCA) is against ostrich farming in Europe stating:

"While domesticated animals such as cattle, sheep, pigs and poultry have been bred and reared specifically as farm animals for many centuries, wild animals have by definition not been domesticated and are often unsuited to a captive farm environment. In addition, there is much less known about the health, husbandry, care and management of non-traditional farm animals which can make it very difficult to meet their needs and provide an adequate standard of welfare".[7]

It should be noted that the RSPCA is opposed to the farming of wild native or introduced animals except when such animals are clearly suitable for farming, or adapt readily to it, can be cared for easily, and can be caught, transported and slaughtered humanely and without causing distress. Farmed ostriches do exhibit abnormal behaviour indicating stress, and concerns have been raised about the transportation of ostriches and slaughter techniques.[21]

Chicken leather

It will surprise many people that chicken skin can be made into serviceable leather but it certainly can. However, finished chicken leather bears little resemblance to chicken skin as we know it from the dining table. Chicken leather is over 1 millimetre thick, (as thick as an emu's), and has a uniquely textured grain pattern with the feather follicles clearly visible.

products that require a degree of 'grip' such as gloves, steering wheel covers or covers for a variety of small items such as mobile phones and wallets. The skin from the legs is also tanned to make small items such as watch straps, key fobs and the like.

Photo 4.6; A full chicken's skin, and inset, skin from a chicken's leg, made into leather

Photo 4.7; Detail from a wallet made from chicken leather

Chickens are farmed of course, they were domesticated over 5,000 years ago and are now the world's most numerous bird. They can reach weights of up to 10 kilograms. The skin can be removed at the abattoir/packaging plant and treated like many other animal skins, initially salted to preserve it. At the tannery, both the flesh and grain side are usually shaved and tanned, dyed and finished in the conventional way.

John Dingle of the University of Queensland's School of Animal Studies has produced a comprehensive report 'Manufacturing Leather from Chicken Skin'.[8] He claims a chicken leather industry is completely viable because, like ostrich leather but to a lesser degree, the quill follicles in chicken leather are a distinctive feature.

Reptile skins
Snakes

At the start of author Paul's 'Understanding Leather' classes at VIA University College, he hands out an unmarked collection of exotic leathers and invites students to guess their origin. One of these is a full size chicken skin. Students rarely identify it as chicken leather, the most popular guess is alligator!

We are all familiar with snake skin. The majority comes from India, (Python and Chera) and Indonesia (Diamond Python and Karung).

Chicken leather is very tough and as durable as any other leather. It is especially good for

Photo 4.8; Snake skin leather

The skins are easily tanned and dyed to produce a leather that is very versatile in terms of patterns and colours. The procedure is relatively straightforward. First, skin your snake! Any flesh is removed and the skin dried. Tanning takes typically 12-24 hours. After tanning the scales are removed, oil applied and the skins dried flat. The skins are softened mechanically and sometimes sanded with abrasive paper. The result is an attractive skin due to the scale pattern.

The collagen fibre structure of snake skin is quite different from that of mammals in that it is horizontal and tightly packed. The result is that the skins, although thin (typically 0.4 millimetres), are relatively tough with medium durability but lacking the softness of mammalian skins.

Snake skin is very much in vogue, being used for footwear, apparel, bags, belts and a whole range of accessories by many of the big fashion brands such as Hermes and Gucci. However there is a number of well-founded concerns about the trade in snake skins.

Pythons are among the most popular snakes used for their skin. All python species are on the CITES Appendix I or II lists, as are boa constrictors, but it is difficult to differentiate between Appendix I or II species once the snake has been skinned and made into leather.

Taking the python trade as an example, there are five species of python traded out of South East Asia where most snake skins used by the fashion industry originate. An estimated 500,000 pythons per year are sourced mainly from Indonesia and Malaysia but also Vietnam, Singapore and Laos. The vast majority make their way to the European fashion houses where the trade is estimated to be worth 1 billion US Dollars annually.

An in-depth analysis of the python trade was carried out by Kasterine and others for the International Trade Centre (ITC) and others in 2012. Their report 'The Trade in South-East Asian Python Skins'[9] raises many areas of concern, specifically about wild life conservation, illegality and corruption, lack of traceability and animal welfare and cruelty. The report concludes that South-East Asian pythons are heavily exploited for their skins, most of which come from the wild rather than sustainable captive breeding on farms. There are strong financial incentives supporting illegal trade and

Photo 4.9; Handbag made from snake skin leather

monitoring and enforcement of regulations is weak. Also criticised are the methods used to slaughter pythons. The report goes on to make a series of recommendations concerning all of the above.

A documentary made by Karl Ammann and Bryan Christy for Journeyman Films in 2011[10] describes the gruesome details behind snakeskin products, and documents the appalling cruelty in the supply chain of snake, lizard and other species in Indonesia on their way to make branded products. Specifically it shows how animals are captured, transported and stored prior to slaughter, involving live skinning in some cases. (Warning - it's very grim viewing!). The film also raises serious issues around the use of endangered species, illegal trade, circumvention of laws, and the need to educate the consumer. There are signs that some in the fashion industry are finally starting to confront these issues. Some of the high fashion brands like Gucci are now collaborating with organisations such as CITES to help establish systems to track skins from 'marsh to market' in an effort to increase transparency and boycott illegal trade.

Kering, a world-leading organisation which is home for multiple powerful brands in the luxury, sports and lifestyle sectors has, in collaboration with The International Union for Conservation of Nature (IUCN) produced a report, sponsored by Gucci, called 'Assessment of Python Breeding Farms Supplying the International High-end Leather Industry'[11]. This supports some of the findings of the previously mentioned ITC report but questions the validity of some of the others, for example concerning captive breeding. The IUCN report makes a series of recommendations including the need for improved data control and monitoring of the industry, more humane killing and tighter certification policies. The report also calls for further research to be done into wild caught versus farmed animals.

Clearly, some fashion brands realize that the situation as it exists today is not sustainable and are taking a proactive approach in making improvements throughout the snake skin trade value chain. Consumers can also help by requesting that retailers provide CITES certification when considering buying exotic leather products, or not buy it at all!

Lizards

Lizard skin produces a versatile, elegant, smooth and luxurious leather some regard to be on a par with crocodile and alligator skin. The skin is usually taken from the belly and is identifiable by the box-like scale pattern. It has a warm 'gloss' and ages well.

Lizards are caught in the wild where the meat is sometimes eaten and the skin goes onto make leather. Several lizard species are used including the Savanah Monitor and the Java Lizard. The tanning process is much like that of snake skin. Lizards are relatively small; there are often only one to two square feet of usable leather per animal. The resulting leather is thin but surprisingly tear resistant making it easy to sew by hand.

The leather is used for a wide range of applications including, boots, shoes, belts, wallets, telephone covers and a variety of luxury goods.

As with snake skin, there are claims that in some cases lizards are skinned alive to make skinning easier and in the belief that this produces a more supple leather; see the section on snake skins, above. According to the Animal Welfare Institute there is a risk that the luxury reptile leather trade is pushing many species towards extinction.[22]

Crocodile and alligator leather

Protected in the wild, these animals are farmed or caught by authorised trapping to produce an easily recognised, high value leather – very tough and durable with high resistance to tearing and abrasion. The meat is sometimes eaten and is white, low in fat and with a mild flavour that some say resembles chicken, (although crocodile meat aficionados firmly state that crocodile meat tastes

Photo 4.10; Lizard leather

Photo 4.11; Crocodile leather briefcase

of crocodile!). Several species are used. Crocodile and alligator leathers are considered classics of the highest quality, and this is reflected in the price. Caiman is an inferior product and is less pliable; also, when creased, cracks will appear between the bony plates, which also prevent even dye penetration.

Animals are collected from a variety of sources including farms and authorised trapping. According to The Animal Welfare Institute, all 23 species of large crocodiles and alligators have been over-exploited by hide hunting, especially in the 1950s and 60s[12]. However such initiatives as CITES protection have allowed some species to recover. Fifteen species of crocodilians are listed on Appendix I of CITES, all other Alligators and Crocodiles are listed on Appendix II allowing trade in some species. Several crocodile species are 'ranched' in many areas of the world.

There are some areas of controversy surrounding the crocodile skin industry. Some experts are of the opinion that a crocodile's biology and behaviour are not suited to captivity of the type seen on farms, claiming that being forced into such close captivity results in a small number of aggressive individual animals dominating the others resulting in stress. In an effort to improve skin quality some farmers use small single pen systems rather than free-range.[13]

When carried out correctly, the animals are dispatched when about 1.5 metres long either by electrocution or by a bullet to the brain. This is not as straightforward as it sounds, a crocodile's brain is about the size and shape of a finger and enclosed in a double brain case. Anything but an exact shot will result in pain and suffering to the animal.

The commercial value of the crocodile lies in its skin. Only a very small percentage of the meat is sold for export; some meat can be sold locally or fed to other crocodiles as they are naturally cannibalistic.

The difference between crocodile and alligator skins

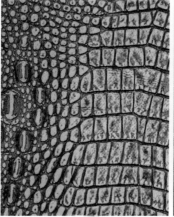

Photo 4.12; Comparison between crocodile (left) and alligator (right) belly scale patterns

Both crocodile and alligator skins have round, square and oblong scales or tiles. Crocodile skins have little dots close to the scale edge. These dots are hair follicles, or sensory pores called integumentary sense organs (ISOs), that assist crocodiles in locating their prey by changes in water pressure. Alligator skins do not have this feature. Another difference is the distribution of the scales. With alligator, the transition from the wide and square shaped scales of the belly to the smaller round shapes of the sides is quite sudden. In crocodile leather this transition is more gradual, with a series of medium-sized scales that slowly become smaller and more rounded.

Two cuts are available; the belly which gives a soft pliable leather with low profile tiles, and the 'hornback' which gives a stiffer leather with a more raised profile. The skins can be tanned with vegetable tanning agents to produce a stiffer product, ideal for luggage, belts and bags. If chrome tanning agents are used, this results in

a more pliable product ideal for footwear and other applications.

A range of finishes is available. The 'classic' finish has a glossy pattern, a 'bombe' finish has a raised tile effect. The 'matt' finish is often applied to hornback cuts and a 'garment' finish is the best for drape and flexibility. A wide variety of colours is possible.

There is also a market in vintage crocodile leather where old skins are recycled to make a wallets, bags, etc.

Fake crocodile leather

Cow leather can be embossed to produce increasingly convincing crocodile copies. The leather is coated with a layer of finish and a steel roller with a crocodile scale pattern presses this pattern into the finished cow leather to produce a more or less convincing fake crocodile leather. (The same technique can be used to make fake snake and lizard skins.) In terms of appearance, these embossed leathers vary from having a plastic-like appearance to looking quite realistic depending on the materials and techniques used. Fake crocodile skin tends to have a repeat pattern unlike the real thing, however some embossed patterns are taken from actual crocodile skins. Another indicator of fake crocodile leather is that the creases between the scales are shiny and not as deep as in the genuine article.

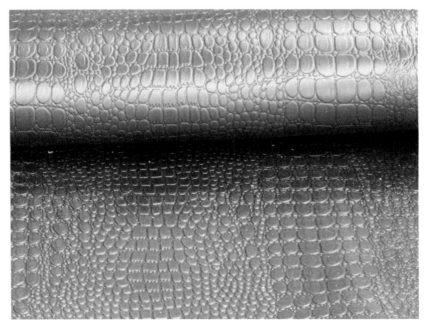

Photo 4.13; Embossed 'crocodile' leather

Amphibians
Frog skin

Frog skin (and toad skin) makes a very interesting leather. The skin usually comes from large bullfrogs caught at night in the Philippines and parts of Indonesia using a strong flashlight and a trident-shaped spear.

The legs can be deep fried and eaten, and are said to 'taste like chicken". We have tried them at several locations around the

world but they only taste of the sauce they are cooked in and the texture is rather different to that of chicken!

The skin can be used to make highly distinctive leather which has a characteristic pattern (and bumps in the case of a toad) which many regard as 'exotic'. The leather is tanned using traditional methods and can be finished in a range of colours. The finished leather has a smooth grain and is surprisingly tough, supple and durable. Applications include a range of small fashion accessories - watch straps, wallets, bags, footwear etc. Prince Charles and Lady Diana were presented with a book bound in cane toad leather by the Premier of Queensland. In the

Photo 4.14; Frogskin leather

Photo 4.15; A cane toad

Philippines the leather is often made into frog-shaped coin purses with a zip located at the base of the abdomen.

In an article in the Guardian 'Why we shouldn't eat frogs' legs',[14] John Henley painted a picture of the frog export industry. Consumption is highest in China, Thailand and Vietnam but frogs are also exported to other countries including France which consumes an estimated 4,000 tonnes of frogs per year, with Indonesia being a major exporter. Originally caught locally, French amphibian populations have been under sharp decline as they have been in many regions of the world due to habitat loss and disease so the French now rely on imports for their traditional delicacy.

Cane Toad leather originates from Australia. In 1935 102 Cane Toads were introduced into the wild in an attempt to control beetles detrimental to sugar cane crops. They have now reached a population estimated to be well in excess of 1 billion and they are now regarded as a pest. The RSPCA recommends as a humane way to kill them, placing the animal in a plastic bag and putting in a refrigerator for 12 hours – this puts the toad to sleep, a further 12 hours in the freezer will kill it.

Back to leather goods, author Paul observed frog leather being made by a farmer in the Philippines using a few buckets of chemicals in his shed. The cost to him of tanning 50 frog skins, which he told me he could easily catch in a few hours hunting at night, was around 6 US dollars. A frog skin ladies bag will set you back at least 400 US dollars!

Sellers of frog skin and frog skin products from Asia often state that the skins are from farmed animals. This is unlikely to be true beyond the practice of small farmers catching frogs on their farms. There has been a number of attempts to farm frogs in Europe and America commercially but the relatively long life cycle of the frog prior to harvesting and disease control have proved too problematic.

As with many exotic species, we lack reliable data on frog and toad population size with respect to the number caught each year for consumption and leather making.

Fish

Fish leather has a long history. Its earliest widespread use appears to be by the Japanese in the 5th century. The Inuit have used fish skin, especially salmon, since the Middle Ages for clothing and footwear. Natives of the Western fjords of Iceland made shoes out of the Atlantic Wolfish and measured the length of journeys by the number of pairs of shoes it took to walk them before wearing out![15]

More recently fish skin has entered the realm of the designer fashion industry as an exotic leather for

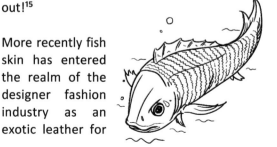

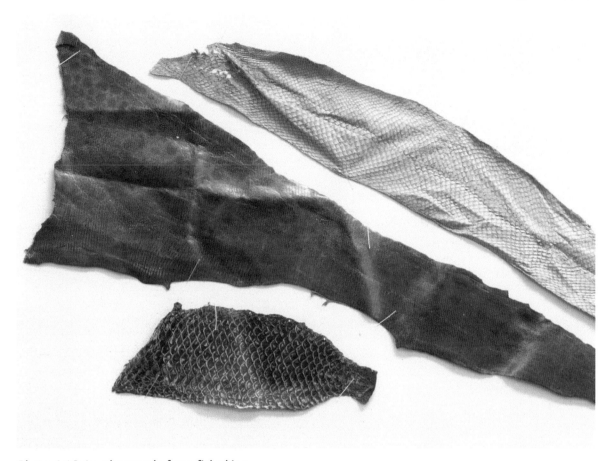

Photo 4.16; Leather made from fish skins

use in clothing, footwear and high end accessories – belts, bags and wallets. Several species of fish are used to make very attractive leathers, strong, durable, supple and aesthetically interesting.

Fish skins are obtained from commercial fisheries and then enter a four to six week process which removes the flesh of the inside of the skin and the scales, which latter can be sold separately to make jewellery and a range of other art and craft products.

An interesting overview of the fish skin tanning industry was given by Julia Bradbury on the BBC programme from 2011 'How fish leather is produced – Kill it, cut it, use it!'.[16] Most fish skin types can be tanned. Atlantic Leather in Iceland makes a range of types of fish leather including salmon, cod and wolf fish, and these find their way into designer goods, bags and footwear for brands such as Guchi, Prada, Dior, Nike and others. Atlantic Leather's Gunnsteinn Bjornsson states that fish leather tanning follows the process of traditional tanning, but fat removal and other tanning processes need to be carried out at lower temperatures to prevent damaging the fish skin. [17] Fish are cold blooded animals and processing at normal tanning temperatures of 35 degrees Celsius or above would result in 'fish soup' being produced.

Make your own exotic leather!

It is possible to make your own fish leather and author Paul followed the method, using salmon skin, suggested by David Boland on the Kingsmere Crafts website.[18] Apparently this is a method also used by the Inuit.

Step 1.   Collect some urine in a bucket and let it stand covered for 24 hours. This apparently brings out the ammonia which will draw out the fat from the skin. Dilute 1:1 with water.

Step 2.   Scrape the flesh off the skin using a blunt instrument, say, the back of a knife. As David Boland suggests, this should be done scraping towards the tail and keeping the skin straight and flat on a supporting board. Paul did not remove the scales at this stage but did trim off the fins.

Step 3.   Allow the skins to sit in the urine for about 18 hours gently agitating occasionally.

Step 4.   Wash the skins using a mild shampoo in warm water. The scales can easily be removed.

Step 5.   Flatten the washed skins on a wooden board, stroking down towards the tail. The skins stick well to the board and fall off when dry usually a day or two.

Step 6.   The skins are now stiff and need to be softened. One way to do this is by working the leather over the edge of a wooden bench. The skins can be dyed using a water soluble leather dye and when dry, treating with leather fat.

The result was a surprisingly tough piece of leather. We are pleased to report that it did not smell of urine but, unlike commercially available fish leather, it did smell faintly of fish!

The fish skins are pickled and tanned using vegetable and chrome tanning agents. They can be finished with a combination of glazes, waxes and resins to produce fish leather in a variety of colours and a variety of textures due to the scale pockets. The resulting leather has surprising strength. The fish leather producers Sea Leather Wear claim on their website that three strips of some fish types woven together can pull an automobile. Our tests on tensile strength indicate that, thickness for thickness, fish skin has at least twice the strength of cow leather. Fish leather is resistant to scratches and stains and is water repellent (no surprises there!) and requires virtually no maintenance. Suede leathers are also available from some species.

Fish leather, if correctly made, does not smell of fish! Interestingly though, cheap, poorly tanned cow leather can – if cheap fish oils are used in the tanning process – but more about this later. The fish species most commonly used include: salmon, carp, bass, sturgeon, shark, catfish, barramundi, stingray and some species of eel. Some of these have some very interesting properties. Leather made from salmon skin has a 'natural memory'; it remembers the original shape of the wearer when used in swimwear for example. Fish leather is used for a variety of

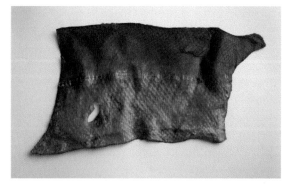

*Photo 4.17; Salmon skin leather made by a student at VIA University, following the recipe in **Make your own exotic leather** on this page*

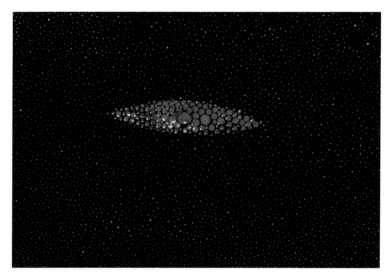

Photo 4.18; Stingray leather

applications including footwear, briefcases, purses, belts, mobile phone cases, etc.

Stingrays (shagreen)

Skingray leather is extremely attractive, easily recognizable, with a surface texture of small hard bumps or pearls, (some refer to it as a 'caviar' effect). The skins have a white, diamond shaped 'crown' at their centre; this is actually made up of calcified scales which are buffed to reveal rounded pale protrusions characteristic to this leather type.

The leather from stingrays and sharks became to be called shagreen around the beginning of the 18th century in Europe, (although shagreen is not strictly leather, it is dried skin rather than tanned). Prior to this, the term shagreen was used for horse leather whose surface had been embedded with plant seeds while soft and removed from the dried skin to achieve a surface with indentations. Stingray's leather is of high strength and durability - up to ten times that of cow leather (this has been confirmed by our own laboratory tests), a fact that caused it to be being

used for body armour in Japan. Also, Samurai sword handles were covered in shagreen due to the leather's non-slip characteristics – useful if the sword handle became slippery with the enemy's blood!

Although naturally highly coloured in life, the colour of the dead fish is a rather dark green and so the skin is re-coloured in the tannery, traditionally to black but many other options are available.

The leather has very high resistance to tearing and is now used to make wallets, briefcases and purses, as well as footwear and apparel. Stingrays are not farmed but caught wild in several parts of South East Asia where the meat is also an important source of protein; stingray leather items are common in these markets. One way of differentiating the real thing from fakes is the red hot needle test - real stingray leather will not puncture. We've tried this and it's true!

They are not regarded as endangered; however, there seems to be little data concerning stingray catches and the Ocean Conservancy has warned in an article 'Stingray Leather: A Fashionable Threat to Species',[19] that any significant increase in demand for stingray leather could threaten several species.

Photo 4.19; Stingray leather purse

Eel skin

Most 'eel skin' does not come from eels at all but from the Pacific Hagfish, an eel-like jawless fish. A by-product of the fishing industry (Sushi), the skin is removed along with the flesh, fat and oils. The skin is tanned then ironed and polished and a waterproofing agent applied. The result is a smooth, supple soft leather, light weight but durable, often with distinctive horizontal stripes. The skins are usually sewn together in panels made in matt or glossy finishes in a range of colours.

Photo 4.20; Eel skin leather purse

Eel skin is used for purses, watchstraps and bags as well as (less often) for clothing, footwear and upholstery.

Sharkskin

A shark's skin is covered with small, sharp 'teeth' called denticles. Untanned skins are sometimes referred to as shagreen, and were used traditionally as a form of sandpaper, in armour, sword hilts and even as a striking surface for matches. The texture of shark skin has provided inspiration for a range of drag reducing and self-cleaning surfaces.[15] The denticles are removed in the tanning process to produce a very tough, durable leather used for wallets, belts, bags and footwear, as well as fashion trips and watch straps. Shark leather is extremely tough. Author Paul's measurements at VIA University College confirm that shark leather's tensile strength can be up to five times stronger than that of cow leather.

Many shark species are considered endangered but not because of the demand for their leather. Rather the problem is shark fin soup which is popular in Asia, especially China, where demand is increasing due to its being regarded as a status symbol. According to Sea Shepherd,[20] an estimated 300 million people consume shark fin soup annually using the fins from around 73 million sharks. The shark's fin is flavourless; its function in soup is only as a thickener. It has been claimed that catches have exceeded sustainable levels for some species. Also the detestable practice of 'shark finning' is on the increase - the fins are usually cut off using a hot knife and the still live shark is thrown back into the sea to bleed to death or drown as the meat

Photo 4.21; Surface of shark skin leather

has little or no value. Shark species affected include Tiger, Lemon, Nurse, Portbeagle, Hammerhead, Mako and Bull sharks.

The popularity of sharkskin could well be due to our fascination with these creatures fuelled by Hollywood movies and a stream of documentary films. Several initiatives have been taken to protect sharks and reduce accidental capture in several parts of the world including the Maldives, South Africa and Australia. Public interest in sharks is fuelling an increasing eco-tourism industry with people wishing to observe sharks in their natural habitats.

Human leather

On a macabre note, we will finish off this chapter by mentioning human leather. A number of libraries have a small number of books in their collection with interesting covers – they are made from human leather. The practice has a name – *Anthropodermic Bibliopegy*. Bookbinding using human leather appears to be quite widely practiced up to around 200 years ago – in particular medical books, for example Tables of the Skeleton and Muscles of the Human Body by Dr John Hunter (1728-1793). Leather made from human skin is said to feature a distinctive pore size and pattern and a waxy smell! [21]

Where did the skins come from? Well, many were medical books so that may provide a clue. The skin came from patients who had no-one to claim their remains or from bodies donated to medical science. Dr John Stockton bound three of his books with the skin of his first trichinosis patent – the inference being to honour people who had furthered medical research.

There are also examples of judicial proceedings being bound with the skin of the murderer convicted and executed in the case. The skin of

Photo 4.22; Arsène Houssay's 19th century book 'Des destinées de l'ame' is bound in human skin

Tests have confirmed that the Houghton Library's copy of Arsène Houssay's 'Des destinées de l'ame' is bound in human skin.

According to the library, Houssaye presented the text, described as "a meditation on the soul and life after death" to Dr Ludovic Bouland, a friend and medical doctor who bound the book with skin of an unclaimed body of a female medical patient who had died of a stroke. Bouland left a note in the volume explaining "a book about the human soul deserved to have a human covering".

(Source: FC8.H8177.879.dc, Houghton Library, Harvard University)

William Burke of Burke and Hare fame executed in 1829 was used to cover a collection of papers concerning the murders. The 1837 memoirs of the notorious highwayman George Walton is another example. He is said to have left the book to one of his victims. The 17th century book about the gunpowder plot conspirator Father Henry Garnet is believed to be bound with the priest's own skin – it is alleged that you see the image of the priest's tortured face on the cover[21].

Libraries and universities accumulate such books through acquisitions and donations and are permitted to keep them for academic research rather than for public display.

> It is said that the 15th century Czech military commander and popular leader of the Hussites - Jan Z Trocnova, ordered on his death-bed that his skin should be tanned and stretched over drums so that he could continue to lead his troops and terrify his enemies after his death!

Ed Gein was an American murderer and grave robber, active in the 1940s and 50s, who took the bodies of recently buried middle aged women home, (he thought they resembled his mother) and tanned their skin to make a range of items including a lampshade and items of clothing. Gein's practice of wearing these items has inspired the creation of several fictional killers including Norman Bates in Psycho and Jame Gumb in The Silence of the Lambs.

Shrunken heads

Most shrunken heads were made by Jivaroan tribes of Equador and Peru. The process starts with removing the skull from the head. A large incision is made at the back of the neck and the skin and flesh removed from the cranium. The eyelids and mouth are pinned or stitched together. The fat is removed and the flesh boiled in water containing a mixture of herbs which are a source of tannin. The skin is dried with hot stones and later hot sand. The whole process shrinks the head to less than a third of its original size. It's a process that requires a high degree of skill and some tribes go to great deal of trouble to retain the features of the victim.

Photo 4.23; A shrunken head

Originally, the preparation of shrunken heads had religious significance but Westerners created an economic demand for shrunken heads and in the late 1800s there was a thriving fake shrunken head industry, although some were not all that fake - they used corpses from morgues. The heads from monkeys and sloths were also used and it has been estimated that the majority of shrunken heads are fakes.

The trade has been banned now but imitation shrunken heads are still readily available, usually made from goatskin or other leather types. Apparently the fakes are distinguishable from the real thing as the stitching is too neat!

In conclusion

The skins from exotic species make very attractive and exclusive leathers, however, a word of caution - greater ethical and environmental awareness among consumers has translated to greater awareness about the treatment of animals and the plight of endangered species and in our view is to be encouraged. If your products contain 'exotic leathers' you can expect probing questions from increasing numbers of consumers. This is less of a problem with fish and some bird leathers, but kangaroo, snakes, lizards and others can be another matter. Stories (and the practice) of snakes and lizards being skinned alive to ensure their softness persist and the use of endangered species is always a real risk and *may* affect consumers' perceptions about you and your products in a negative way.

Chapter 4 references:

1. Doward, J. (06/12/2011). [On-line]. *"Record" number of thoroughbreds being slaughtered for meat.* Available at: www.theguardian.com. Accessed: 13/12/2013.

2. Nestle, M. (19 February 2013). [On-line]. *The horse meat scandal – an object lesson in food politics.* Available at: www.foodpolitics.com. Accessed on 11/10/2014. (Note not the brand Nestlé).

3. World Horse Welfare News. (Summer 2012). *Transportation campaign update.* World Horse Welfare.

4. Humane Society International. (n.d.) [On-line]. *Horse Transport & Slaughter.* Available at: www.hsi.org. Accessed: 28/04/2014.

5. Gellatley, J. (n.d.). [On-line]. *A Viva! Report on ostrich farming.* Available at: www.viva.org.uk. Accessed: 04/09/2015.

6. Poulter, S. (04/09/2012). [On-line]. *Kangaroo gets the boot from Adidas.* Available at: www.dailymail.co.uk. Accessed: 12/03/2014.

7. RSPCA. (2008). [On-line]. *Ostrich Farming.* Available at: www.rspca.org.uk. Accessed: 11/11/2014.

8. Dingle, J. (2001). *Manufacturing Leather from Chicken Skin.* Rural Industries Research & Development Corporation.

9. Kasterine, A., Arbeid, R., Caillabet, O. and Natusch, D. (2012). *The Trade in South-East Asian Python Skins.* International Trade Centre (ITC), Geneva.

10. Ammann, K. (2011). *The gruesome details behind snakeskin purses.* Documentry – Journeyman Pictures. http://journeyman.tv/62548/short-film.

11. Natusch, D.J.D. and Lyons, J.A. (2014). *Assessment of python breeding farms supplying the international high-end leather industry.* A report under the 'Python Conservation Partnership' programme of research. Occasional Paper of the IUCN Species Survival Commission No. 50. Gland, Switzerland: IUCN. 56pp.

12. Animal Welfare Institute. (2011). [On-line]. *Skins of Suffering: Fashion trade falls hard on reptiles.* Available at: https://awionline.org. Accessed: 04/01/2015.

13. Warwick, C. (5. October 2006). [On-line]. *Crocodile Farms: is it cruel to keep these wild creatures captive?* Available at: www.independent.co.uk. Accessed 10/10/2014.

14. Henley, J. (2009). *Why we shouldn't eat frogs legs.* Available at: www.theguardian.com. Accessed: 05/06/2014.

15. Ehrlich, H. (2015). *Biological Materials of Marine Origin: vertebrates.* Springer Dordrecht Heidelberg, New York, London.

16. BBC. (2011). *How fish leather is produced (mors fish leather sneakers). Kill it cut it, use it.* Hosted by Julia Bradbury. Available at: https://www.youtube.com/watch?v=i20MaVfqJl4. Accessed: 01/02/2014.

17. Bjornsen, G. (2013). *Fish Leather Tanning.* Email dated: 29/10/2013.

18. Boland, D. (n.d.). [On-line]. *How Leather is Produced: tanning fish skins.* Available at: www.kingsmerecrafts.com/page08.html. Accessed: 11/05/2013.

19. Ocean Conservancy (The). (n.d.). [On-line]. *Stingray Leather: A fashionable threat to species.* Available at: http:// act.oceanconservancy.org. Accessed: 05/05/2015.

20. Sea Shepherd. (n.d.). *The Brutal Business of Shark Finning.* Available at: www.seashepherd.org. Accessed: 18/03/2015.

21. Veronese, K. (2012). *Anthropodemic Bibliopegy, of the Truth about Books Bound in Human Skin.* Available at: http://io9.com. Accessed on 30/05/2015.

22. Wotton S B & Hewitt L (1999). *Transportation of Ostriches - A Review.* Vet. Rec. 1999; 145: 725-731. Pmid:10972110.

23. Animal Welfare Institute. (n.d.). [On-line]. *Endangered Species Handbook.* Available at: www.endangeredspecieshandbook.org. Accessed: 11/10/2014.

Chapter 4 photographs:

4.1. Inna Felker, Dreamstime.com

4.2. Inge Hogenbijl, Dreamstime.com

4.3, 4.6, 4.8, 4.10, 4.11, 4.13, 4.14, 4.16, 4.17, 4.18, 4.21, 4.23, M G Mirams & P J McElheron

4.4. Hel080808, Dreamstime.com

4.5. Igor Strukov, Dreamstime.com

4.7. By kind permission of Exoticleather.biz

4.9. Tatyana Gladskikh, Dreamstime.com

4.12. Amnarj2006/Morganka, Dreamstime.com

4.11. Extezy, Dreamstime.com

4.15. Mgkuijpers, Dreamstime.com

4.19. Nikolay Razumov, Dreamstime.com

4.20. Athina Psoma, Dreamstime.com

4.22. By kind permission of The Houghton Library, Harvard University.

CHAPTER 5, LEATHER FINISHES

In this chapter we cover the different types of finishes used with leather. A 'finish' is something you apply to (or do to) the surface of the leather. There is a wide range of leather finishing techniques, both chemical and mechanical. This chapter will discuss the features of the most used finish types, why they are used and what are their relative strengths and weaknesses.

Almost all leather is dyed through. The natural colour of leather can be grey, sometimes light brown, and usually with significant colour variation across the skin. The majority of leathers are 'finished'; that is to say, the surface is treated in some way, often sprayed with a mixture of chemical materials or treated mechanically at the end of the leather making process. Leathers are finished for a variety of reasons:

- To enhance the natural beauty of the leather.

- To provide some protection to the leather – against water, sunlight, wear, scuffing etc.

- To Increase utilisation by masking defects and colour variation.

- To provide certain aesthetic characteristics, colour, pattern, texture etc.

- To impart some special property, waterproofness, chemical resistance, touch, feel etc.

Finishing leather is a highly specialised operation often requiring a great deal of expertise, and finishes are a complex mixture of pigments, dyes, binding agents, polymers and auxiliaries. The particular composition and application will depend on the requirements of the finished leather, not only in terms of the colour but also gloss, handle, water or solvent resistance, flexibility, flex or scuff resistance, etc. Finishing can also take the form of some mechanical action such as buffing suede or nubuck. Some

full grain leathers are required to have a natural look and as a consequence are virtually unfinished.

> **Grain leather.** The grain refers to the pattern on the surface of the leather, characterised by the pores and hair follicles peculiar to the animal concerned. Grain leather has the surface layer substantially intact and is finished on the grain side.

Most leathers used to make footwear, furniture and apparel etc. fall into one of four general categories. For full explanations of the terms used, see later in this chapter or the Glossary of Leather Terms at the end of this book.

Full-grain leathers are those where the grain surface has not been sanded, buffed, or snuffed (as opposed to top-grain or corrected leather) to remove imperfections (marks, scratches etc.) on the surface of the hide. The grain remains intact. Full grain leathers can develop a patina in time adding to their aesthetic appeal. Full grain leathers are used in high quality leather furniture and footwear and are typically available in two finish types: **aniline** and **semi-aniline**.

Top-grain leather (a common type used in high-end leather products) is the second-highest quality. It has had the 'split' layer separated away, making it thinner and more pliable than full-grain. Its surface has been sanded and a finish coat added to the surface which results in a colder, plastic feel with less breathability, and it will not develop a natural patina. It is typically less expensive and has greater resistance to stains than full-grain leather.

Corrected-grain leather is any leather that has had an artificial grain applied to its surface. The hides used to create corrected leather do not meet the standards for use in creating vegetable-tanned or aniline leather. The imperfections are 'corrected' or sanded off before a finish is applied; an artificial grain may be embossed into the surface and dressed with stain or dyes. Most corrected-grain leather is used to make pigmented leather as the solid pigment helps hide the corrections or imperfections. Another variation is more lightly finished, resembling semi-aniline leather. (See later in this chapter for more details.)

Split leather is created from the fibrous part (corium) of the hide left once the top-grain of the raw hide has been removed. During the splitting operation, the top-grain and bottom split are separated. The bottom split can be further split (thickness allowing) into a middle split and a flesh split. Split leather can then have then an artificial layer applied to the surface of the split which may be embossed with a leather grain. Splits are also used to create suede leather.

Let's discuss the main finish types in detail.

Aniline finish

 *With an aniline finish, the grain is fully exposed.*

This is a full grain leather that has been dyed using aniline dyestuffs only. The leather is sometimes given a light polymer finish treatment but without the application of pigments. This finishing may be in the form of a light mechanical polishing or glazing. In this case, the tips of the grain surface burnish to a slightly darker shade which gives a very attractive 'rich' or 'natural' look. The grain is not covered with any opaque finishes. Any fat lines, neck wrinkles, colour variation defects etc. are visible and the 'open pores', indicating where the hairs were situated, are clearly visible under a magnifying glass. The aim with aniline leather is to achieve a natural leather look with the grain clearly visible. With time, aniline leather can develop a very attractive patina. An advantage is that the lack of finish on the surface allows the leather to breathe, which aids comfort which is of course especially important in footwear. Aniline leathers also adjust to body temperature quickly adding to seating comfort. Producing aniline leathers is only possible with materials that have an even grain surface, relatively free from defects and without colour variation. Consequently, only the best leathers can be used to make aniline leather - only around five percent of leathers are of adequate quality. Consistency in manufacture can also be a problem and these factors are reflected in the price of aniline leathers, which are comparatively expensive.

The disadvantages inherent with aniline leather are that it is not protected with a surface finish and so may fade in direct sunlight or be

Photo 5.2; A sofa made from aniline Leather

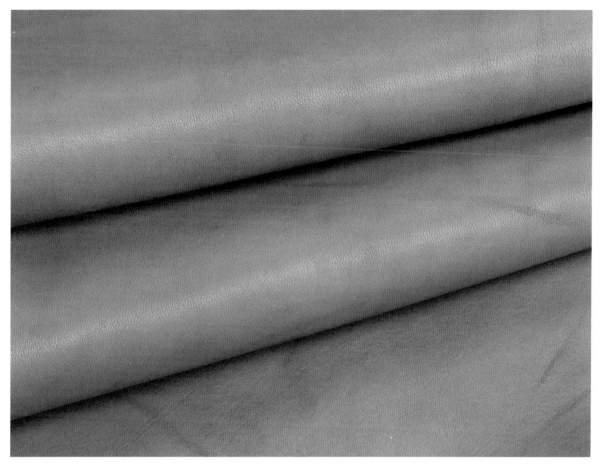

Photo 5.1; Aniline Leather

susceptible to staining from spillages and soiling from grease and perspiration. In order to reduce these problems a very light finish containing micro pigments may be applied which partially masks any colour variation and offers a degree of protection against fading and staining. This is referred to as 'protected aniline' or 'aniline plus'. Designers love aniline leather; it is soft to the touch and has a 'natural look' as the leather is in its natural dyed state. It is used especially for footwear, apparel and furniture.

How to identify aniline leathers

The natural grain surface is plainly visible and obviously free of heavy finish treatment. There may be some colour variation across the skin. Scratch the leather with a thumbnail – if it scratches to a lighter colour, this indicates aniline leather. Add a drop or two of water to the scratched surface – if it is quickly absorbed this is further confirmation of an aniline finish.

Semi-aniline finish

With semi-aniline finish, the grain is exposed, but has a thin protective or corrective layer.

Most leathers have faults in terms of variation in grain and/or colour across the skin, and the presence of scratches, insect bites, and so on. This is undesirable for many applications as consumers do not want to see colour or grain variation within a pair of shoes or over a garment or sofa, for example. One solution is to apply a light coat of finish with sufficient opacity to mask any slight colour variation but without hiding the natural grain of the leather. Such finishes are called semi-aniline.

Semi-aniline leather is a full grain leather to which a light surface finish coating containing a small amount of pigment has been applied. This provides a degree of durability and stain resistance without hiding the natural grain of the leather. Semi-aniline is more durable than true aniline leather and the raw material quality requirements in terms of grain and colour variation are not quite so high. Approximately

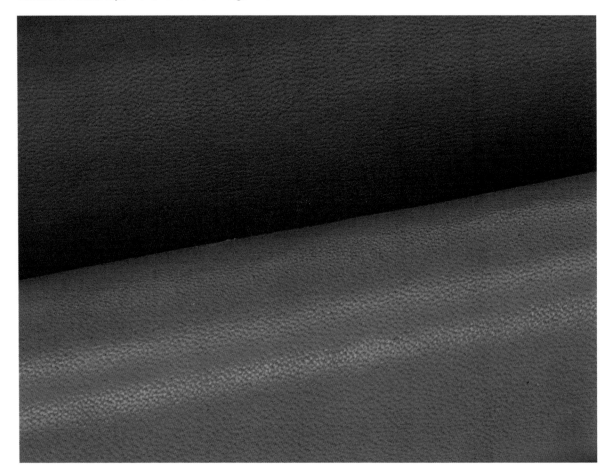

Photo 5.3; Comparing aniline leather (top) with semi-aniline

15 percent of the most common types of leather are finished as semi-aniline.

The additional finish does impart a slight plastic-looking sheen to the surface of the leather which is a move away from the fully natural aniline look. However, carefully done, semi-aniline leathers retain the appearance of high quality leathers and are a commercial alternative to pure aniline finishes. The increased protection against fading in sunlight, water damage and wear generally means that semi-aniline leathers are a good compromise between quality and cost. The pores are still visible under a magnifying glass but are not as 'open' as with aniline leathers.

Pigmented full grain leather

 *Pigmented finish requires a heavier layer of material to mask surface detail*

In this case, a resin based pigmented spray is applied to the surface of the leather. As for identification, it is still possible to see that it is leather, but any surface detail is masked by what is essentially a thin polymer film.

The disadvantages are that heavily pigmented leathers can have somewhat of an artificial look

Photo 5.4; Pigmented full-grain leather

relative to aniline leather, and the grain surface is masked in part by the pigment. However, pigmented finished leather still looks like leather (if it is lightly pigmented), and has very good light fastness, good resistance to staining and is easy to clean. The colour and surface appearance are very uniform. Pigmented leathers can look very attractive, for example almost all automobile leathers are pigmented or corrected grain leathers. The in-car environment is one where light fading would be likely with lightly or unfinished leathers; also car manufacturers demand that the leather in all cars throughout the production run has the same appearance and colour.

The reduced breathability of pigmented leather is sometimes compensated for by perforating the leather with small holes, often incorporated into a pattern in the seat contact regions. It's also about fitness for purpose; pigmented leathers might be a better choice than aniline for families with small children or for restaurants etc.

Pigmented leathers will not develop a patina over time. Pigmented leathers are less expensive than aniline and semi-aniline leathers as lower grades of leather (those with more in the way of defects and colour variation) can be used.

Photo 5.5; Pigmented corrected grain leather

Corrected grain leather

If the grain surface on leather is coarse and lacking uniformity, then it can be 'corrected'. This involves buffing the surface of the grain with a fine sandpaper and then applying a new chemical surface finish to the leather. Often an imitation grain print is embossed into the leather surface. While corrected grain leathers, sometimes referred to as 'top grain leathers', do not have the natural appearance of aniline or semi aniline leathers, they are soft, strong, hardwearing and durable. Corrected grain leathers are good commercial leathers, well protected against sunlight, water and spills and are widely used for clothing, furniture, automotive and footwear applications. They are sometimes used to make 'pigmented' leather. 'Aniline corrected grain' is also available where a light finish is applied to a corrected grain material and this can look very attractive.

Finished splits

Cattle leathers are too thick for most applications and are split using a band knife

Photo 5.6; A split leather finished with a polyurethane film (a 'PU split')

splitting machine to produce two (or sometimes more) separate layers or 'splits'. A 'grain split', which has the grain surface of the leather intact, can be finished using any of the above methods. A 'flesh split' consists of the corium and the flesh side; flesh splits can be buffed to produce a nap and become suede leathers. Flesh splits can also be sprayed with a surface coating to resemble grain leather. They may also be embossed with a variety of patterns or have a film laminated on their surface to produce patent leather.

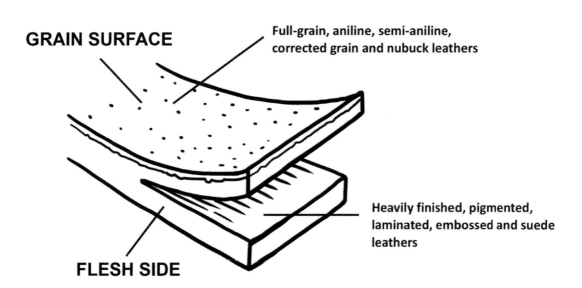

GRAIN SURFACE

Full-grain, aniline, semi-aniline, corrected grain and nubuck leathers

Heavily finished, pigmented, laminated, embossed and suede leathers

FLESH SIDE

Thicker leather can be split into three (or even more) layers. The strength of the resulting splits is dependent on thickness and the entanglement of their collagen fibres. This level of entanglement decreases as one moves further from the grain towards the flesh side so articles manufactured from bottom splits thinner than one millimetre require reinforcement.

It is not uncommon to find furniture with the more visible 'contact areas' made from a high quality leather, and side and back panels made from splits finished to match the better quality leather in colour and grain appearance.

Suede

The term 'suede' is thought to come from the French: 'gants de Suede' meaning 'gloves of Sweden'. A process of abrasive action called buffing raises the corium fibres to produce an even, short fibre or 'nap' finish. Suede leather is finished with a raised nap by buffing the flesh-side surface. This can be the flesh side of the grain split leather, or either surface of a flesh split. Suedes are attractive, tough leathers, finding wide application in the footwear, furniture, apparel, bags, accessories and glove sectors.

In bovine leathers, the collagen fibres in the corium are coarse in nature, relative to those in sheep, goat and pig leathers. The resulting suede nap is therefore coarser compared with the nap obtained when buffing non-bovine material, which can produce fine suede (akin to nubuck, see below).

Identifying suede: the nap does not 'finger mark' or show a 'two way rub' or 'writing effect' (as is the case with nubuck, see below), as the suede fibres are quite springy and rebound quickly to the original upright position.

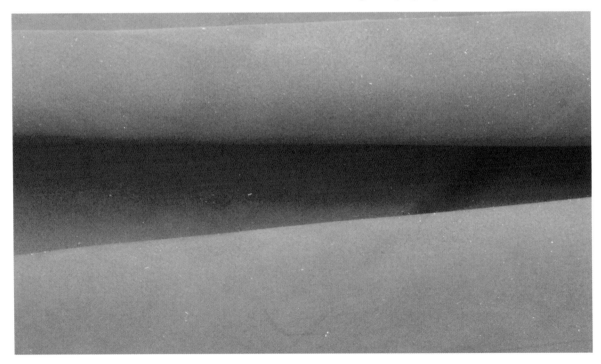

Photo 5.7; Suede, made from the flesh side of a full thickness leather or split

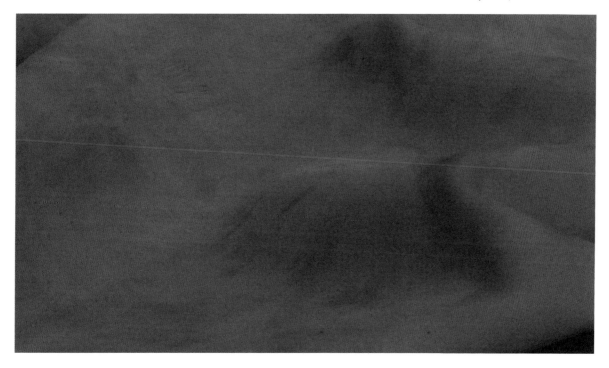

Photo 5.8; Nubuck, made from the grain side of a full-thickness leather or split

Nubuck

Nubuck leathers, (the term is thought to originate from 'new buckskin'), sometimes referred to as velvet suedes, are made by buffing the grain surface of the leather. This process is often referred to as 'snuffing' which is a term to denote a finer buffing. As the collagen fibres are finer in the grain than in the corium, the result is a finer nap than is the case with suede. The nap is then brushed or plush wheel padded to produce a velvety, lustrous appearance and feel. Wax, grease or oil toppings are sometimes applied to give an appealing effect. These leathers are termed oil nubucks.

How to identify nubucks

Available in a wide range of colours they have a fine velvety nap on the grain side. They possess what is known as a 'writing effect'; that is to say you can write on the surface with your finger and the impression stays.

Nubuck is more expensive than suede as grain leather is used and, even though the surface is snuffed, the leather still needs to be of good quality and free from defects.

Nubucks are used mainly in the footwear and furniture industries.

Embossed leather

If finished leather is pressed against a hard, hot, raised patterned metal plate, the surface fibre structure of the leather will retain an impression so that, on release, it holds a mirror image of the plate. It is a property of leather that has been known for hundreds of years and opens up many

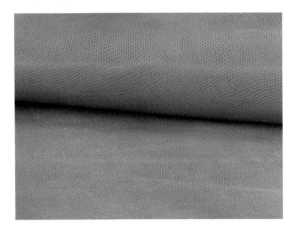

Photo 5.9; An embossed leather with a lizard skin effect

possibilities. Leathers can be embossed with crocodile, lizard and snake effects as well as an infinite range of other patterns. Sometimes actual crocodile and other skins are used as the 'master' for making the embossing dies which can result in some very realistic embossed leathers.

The softer the leather, the easier is it to emboss, but the embossing is less permanent. Experience shows that the embossing of leather with a moisture content of 14-16 percent becomes more permanent, especially if higher temperatures are involved.

Photo 5.10; Embossed leather is popular for handbags

Vegetable tanned leathers are usually easier to emboss as they retain the impression pattern better than the more elastic chrome tanned leathers. However, good results can be achieved with chrome leathers if higher temperatures, pressures and dwell times are used. Embossing tends to make the leather firmer but adjustments can be made in the process to counteract this.

Embossing pigmented leathers can serve to hide many of the defects occurring in leather such as scratches and insect bites etc. Also, the many attractive effects are possible at relatively low cost. Lower grade leathers can be used and a crocodile, (or any other endangered species), does not have to be culled in order to make a 'crocodile' effect handbag! Disadvantages include the fact that embossed leather can look cheap and plastic-like if not done well, however very realistic effects can be achieved. The leathers tend to be quite firm and stiff – an advantage for many handbag designs but a problem for many other applications. Also breathability is compromised; not a problem for some applications but can be so for footwear. Embossed leathers are commonly used for belts, footwear, bags etc.

Pull-up leather (waxy/oil pull-up)

This refers to a leather that has additional oil added to it during manufacture and then sprayed on the surface together with wax as part of the finish operation. This gives the leather a dark, almost greasy, look and feel. This is not as bad as it sounds and the effect can be very pleasing as it imparts a rugged outdoor look. The finish is designed to lighten when stressed or stretched which results in an interesting worn-in effect. Pull-up leather is similar to nubuck and suede in that the material does not have a protective

Photo 5.11; Pull-up leather

coating of finish applied to it. It is prone to colour change in areas of high wear and can transfer colour to clothing in some cases.

Pull-up leathers are associated with 'high quality' and have good water resistance and are used for bags, upholstery and outdoor footwear.

Dry milled leather

To achieve this effect the leather is loaded into a milling drum and rotated. The soft falling action intensifies the natural lines in the leather to give an attractive 'pebbling' effect. In addition, dry milling makes the leather considerably softer.

Dry milling is also one of the techniques to make vegetable tanned leathers softer.

Photo 5.12; The surface of a dry milled leather

Photo 5.13; An antique-effect leather sofa

Antique grain (two-tone leather)

These are varieties of pigmented leathers where the surface is given an interesting 'antique' effect by applying a top coat which is applied unevenly or partially removed to reveal a contrasting underlying colour coat. The leather may have had hollows or creases embossed in its surface prior to the application of the two colour coats, so the first coat, usually the darker one, settles in the depressions created by the embossing. The effect, which is designed to give a worn or patina appearance, can be very attractive and relies on the very thin top layer having limited durability, and the leather being subject to colour change during life. Antique leathers are used in furniture applications.

Laminated leather, PU leather

Flesh (or middle) leather splits are made more attractive, and therefore have the possibilities for their applications widened, by laminating the surface with coloured, patterned and/or protective layers, usually of polyurethane. These leathers were originally developed for the footwear industry but have also been used by the furniture industry and for bags etc. The leathers will not improve with age as is the case with many leather types used for furniture applications; they will not become more supple or develop any kind of patina. There is also the slight risk that the polyurethane layer will delaminate in use.

One of the main advantages of leather finished in this way is price. Lower grade splits can be used to produce shiny leathers which retain a like-new appearance for long periods and are easy to maintain and clean. Any breathability is lost however. Although the finished material often has very little of the true characteristics of leather in terms of grain, colour, porosity or feel, manufacturers and retailers are able to sell furniture, footwear and accessory items made from laminated leather as 'leather' or even 'genuine leather' products!

Photo 5.14; Low-value split leathers laminated with coloured polyurethane layers

Patent leather

Patent leather was first made commercially by Seth Boyden in 1818 when he applied linseed oil based products to leather to produce a high gloss finish. Its name was derived from the fact that some of the original processes that were further developed by Boyden were covered by patents. Patent leather became popular as dress or evening shoes as it could be readily distinguished from work footwear, and later went on to become the standard wear for dancing shoes.

Modern 'patent' leather either has a liquid resin coating applied to the surface to give the high gloss, or, at the popular end of the market, is more likely to be made by the application of a layer of plastic material laminated to the surface of the leather (see Laminated Leather, above).

Photo 5.15; A 'patent' look - genuine or laminated?

Glazed finish

Aniline leathers can be polished with an agate stone (or using a steel or glass block) to achieve a glazed, polished surface. Occasionally a varnish is applied. The technique is used on cow leather and kidskins.

Other finish effects

Metalised leather: Leather given a metallic lustre by the application of a metallic foil to the surface of the leather.

Printed leather: Leather with a surface pattern achieved by embossing or by press printing, foils, or screen printing.

Photo 5.16; Screen-printed leather

Perforated leather: Leather perforated with small holes, usually in some form of pattern. They are widely used in the automotive industry to achieve air flow and improved seat ventilation allowing pigmented leathers to be more comfortable in warm temperatures or when skin comes into direct contact with the leather.

Recap of terms

Full grain leather, top grain leather, genuine leather, bonded leather – what's the difference?

The above terms are frequently used and can be very confusing, so, in summary, the following should give clarity:

Full grain leather is leather of the highest quality with the grain intact and untreated by buffing, sanding etc.

Top grain leather covers **corrected grain leathers** where the leather has been lightly sanded to remove scars and defects etc. **Pigmented leather** is often made from corrected grain leather.

Genuine leather covers leathers which don't have any grain and are made from flesh splits, and can include suedes, embossed and laminated leathers.

Bonded leather is not really leather at all. It's the dust, trimmings and shavings of the leather bonded together with latex or similar material and pressed together. So-called genuine and bonded leathers are often treated to look like full or top grain leather. Bonded leather does not have the strength or durability of 'real' leather.

Chapter 5 photographs:

5.1, 5.3 - 5.12 inclusive, 5.14, 5.16. M G Mirams & P J McElheron.

5.2. Marko Bradic, Dreamstime.com

5.13. Sergei Razvodovskij, Dreamstime.com

5.15. Tatsiana Shypulia, Dreamstime.com

CHAPTER 6, HOW LEATHER IS MADE

In this chapter we describe how leather is made and how the tanning process operates - provide you with a process for making your own leather. We cover the two main tanning (vegetable and chrome tanning) in some detail, discussing the differences and merits of briefly touch on other methods.

Setting the scene: do-it-yourself tanning

Imagine finding yourself in a situation where you have managed to trap and kill an animal, say a goat. After you've polished off the meat you might wish to make some leather. This is relatively straightforward; here's how you would go about it:

Step one: Remove the skin from the animal and put the animal's brain on one side – you'll be using it later. Scrape any meat and other mesentery adhering to the flesh side (this is called fleshing in the tannery).

Step two: Soak the skin in an alkali solution. This you can make from wood ash which contains potassium hydroxide - add water to the ashes to make a solution of milkshake-like consistency. Place the skin in the solution and weigh it down with stones, cover and leave for two to three days. The reason for doing this is to remove mucous and unwanted inter-fibrillary proteins from the skin and to facilitate oil and fat penetration later. It will also swell the skin and make it easier to remove the hair, if required.

Step three: Scrape away the hair using a knife or improvised scraper. There is actually a bit of a knack to doing this but by the time you have scraped away all the hair you will probably have acquired it!

Steps two and three would be called liming and de-hairing in the tannery

Step four: All alkalinity and swell must be removed and this can be done by soaking the skin in water along with a little acid (for example vinegar) if you have it. Soaking overnight will do it.

Step five: Dressing - wring out the skin to remove all excess moisture and prepare a dressing solution. You can use the animal's brain premixed in hot water to make a solution of soup-like consistency. Soak the skin in the dressing solution. You might wish to accelerate the soaking process by stretching the skin periodically. After a soaking time of 12 hours or so, wring out the hide, taking care to catch and reuse your dressing solution. Repeat the soaking and wringing process.

Step six: Softening - the technique here is to continually move, stretch and realign the fibres of the hide as you go from damp to dry. Several constituents of the hide behave like glue, locking the collagen fibres together and producing a stiff board. By stretching and manipulating the skin, you will prevent this from happening. It is also necessary to buff both the flesh and the grain sides of the leather as the leather dries to prevent crust formation that will stiffen the

In his book Deer Skins Into Buck Skins, Matt Richards[1] suggests that, instead of brains, you can use a dozen eggs or a small bar of soap and a little neat's-foot oil (oil rendered from the shin and foot bones of cattle and used to soften and preserve leather), to make a dressing solution.

r. This process might take two to four
urs.

> The term *tanning* is derived from the medieval Latin word *tannare* – 'to dye a tawny colour' which is a derivative of *tannum* (crushed oak bark), an original source of tannin.[2]

The reason for going through this primitive tanning process is to illustrate the basic steps in leather making as it has been carried out for thousands of years and up until the present day

in some areas of the world. As you would imagine though, scaling up the process to commercial quantities, plus years of research and development, have resulted in a few refinements resulting in the modern industrial tanning process, and it is this that we discuss now.

How does leather tanning work?

In life, an animal's skin is soft and flexible as the protein fibres that make up skin are able to move in relation to each other. If an animal is skinned and the skin (raw-hide) is left untreated, it will either dry out to become hard and stiff or, if it remains in a wet state, will be attacked by bacteria and will rot in a short time. The aim of the tanning process at its most basic is to retain the animal skin's natural properties, producing a leather that is soft, flexible and supple when dry, and resistant to rotting when wet.

Skin consists of interwoven fibres made from the protein collagen. As a raw hide skin dries out, these collagen fibres shrink and bond together to produce a rigid structure. So the tanning operation must stabilise the structure of the collagen fibres, keeping them apart by treating them chemically and lubricating them so they can move relative to each other. There are some other properties we

> The word collagen is derived from the Greek **Kolla**, meaning glue, and **gen**, meaning 'that which produces'.[3] A strong glue can be produced by boiling animal skins and sinews in water.

Photo 6.1; A modern tannery is clean, efficient and highly mechanised

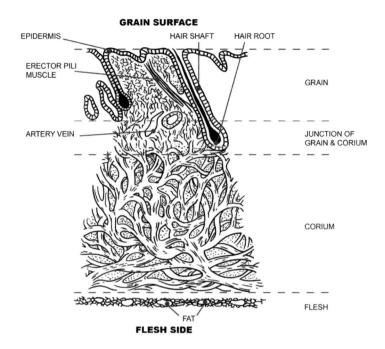

GRAIN SURFACE

EPIDERMIS

ERECTOR PILI MUSCLE

ARTERY VEIN

HAIR SHAFT   HAIR ROOT

GRAIN

JUNCTION OF GRAIN & CORIUM

CORIUM

FLESH

FAT

FLESH SIDE

Cross-section of cow leather, showing the structure

expect from leather - toughness, strength, durability and 'breathability' along with several aesthetic characteristics such as touch, colour and finish and these can be achieved in the tanning process.

Tanning is the term used for the process of converting an animal's hide or skin into leather. This is usually done by soaking or steeping the

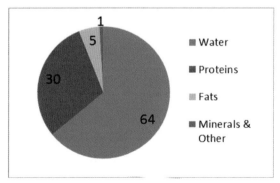

1
5
30
64

■ Water
■ Proteins
▥ Fats
■ Minerals & Other

Typical composition of an animal's skin or hide (percent)

hide in a strong solution of vegetable extracts (tannins) for several weeks (or tanning in drums in the presence of tannin and enzymes) or, in the more commonly used chrome tanning, by tumbling the skins in a water solution containing chrome in large drums for several hours.

To understand how the tanning process works, we need to know something about the structure of leather. As pointed out in a previous chapter, fresh skins and hides removed from the animal consist of water (a lot of water – over 60 percent), proteins (around 30 percent), fatty material and some mineral salts (about six percent). The most important constituent from the material point of view is the protein collagen and this is all that is remaining in finished leather after the other original material (apart from some of the water) is removed in the tanning process. Finished leather is essentially made up of numerous collagen fibre bundles intimately interwoven to form a strong, tough, flexible, permeable structure.

Collagen is the protein that makes up skin (and eventually leather) and is a long chain of molecules twisted together in threes to form a helix, rather like a rope. During the tanning process chemical bonds hold the molecules together so they bundle up to form collagen microfibrils. These in turn combine to form

A nanometre is one billionth of a metre (0.000000001 metres). A micron is one millionth of a metre (0.000001 metres, or 1000 nanometres). The width of a human hair is about 100 microns.

fibrils (typically 100 nanometers in diameter). Fibrils further combine to form fibres one micron in diameter. These fibres group together into bundles organised in a complex network structure which is just about visible to the naked eye if you look at a piece of leather in cross-section.[3]

The structure of the collagen fibres is very much like that of a hemp rope

The analogy with a hemp rope is a useful one. The strength of the rope depends on the strength of the individual fibres and the way they are twisted together. Also, wetting a rope causes swelling of the individual fibres which tightens the twist of the fibres.

There is a lot of water in raw hide, above 60 percent, half of which is held as 'free water' between the collagen fibres and about a further quarter is chemically bound to the collagen protein. This water in effect holds the collagen protein molecules apart, and, when it is removed through drying, the long fiberous molecules shrink closer together as the skin dries and chemical bonds on the collagen fibres, previously used to hold the water, bond with one another. This results in a harder, rigid structure which contributes to the hardness and lack of flexibility of the dried hide. Note that the loss of free water does not result significantly in the hardening effect; it is when the final 25 percent is removed that we observe hardening. One of the main objectives of the tanning process is to prevent this hardening occurring so the leather remains flexible and supple when dry.[4]

The tanning process at its most basic does two things:

1. In the preparation phase, the skin is cleaned, de-haired and any impurities in the skin such as unwanted proteins are removed, leaving a collagen fibre network.

2. Tanning agents (usually vegetable or chromium based) are added to hides, and these materials, depending on their chemical nature, are thought to partially fill the spaces between the collagen fibres and, in the case of chrome, forming cross-links within the collagen structure.[5]

Vegetable tanning

Vegetable tanning really does merit the term 'tanning' as it is the only process that employs tannin, or tannic acid, to make leather.[6] This is the oldest form of tanning but still used today for applications where firmness, mouldability or the ability to retain an embossed or tooled pattern, are required. Vegetable tanning agents are extracted from certain types of plant leaves and barks. The active ingredient is tannin and it occurs to a greater or lesser degree in most forms of plant life. The choice of tannin source traditionally would depend on what was available, oak for example in much of Europe, but now tannin extracts from more effective exotic sources can be used. The colour imparted to the leather will vary from light brown to dark reds and the firmness and hardness of the finished leather will vary according to the tannin source chosen. Another property of relevance is astringency, which determines the rate at which the tan combines with the collagen fibres. Popular sources of tannin still include oak bark, chestnut wood, pine bark, but also mangrove bark, mimosa bark, (from Australia, Brazil and

Africa) and quebracho wood (from South America).

> pH - A measure of acidity, with strong acids having a low value near zero and strong alkalis a value towards the maximum of 14.0. Pure water is pH 7.0

Acidic groups in the vegetable tannins combine with basic groups in the collagen protein displacing the water. When the leather is dried, the coating of vegetable tan molecules on the collagen fibres interferes with their ability to bond together.[7] The softness of the finished leather depends in part on the type and quantity of the vegetable tans used. A vegetable tanned leather can contain up to 50 percent of vegetable tanning material and this contributes to the stiffness of the leather. Also, it takes some considerable time to get this amount of vegetable tanning materials to bond to the collagen; tanning times were traditionally very long, typically several months, although this time has later been much reduced with the introduction of more concentrated tanning extracts, the control of pH, mechanical agitation (drums rather than pits) and the use of enzymes.

Photo 6.2; Most of the tanning processes are nowadays carried out in large wooden rotating drums

The vegetable tanning process

The vegetable tanning process is different from chrome tanning in several respects. Following the removal of any remaining flesh, and soaking in a lime solution to remove the hair, the hides are stretched on frames and immersed in vats of increasing concentrations of tannin for a period of several weeks and observed regularly. Tanning using drums is also possible, a process that takes a few days. After the tanned hides have been sorted for quality they may be washed and bleached or aniline dyed in drums for 10 hours, the wet hides are pressed to eliminate excess water. The tanning process so far has removed the natural fat from the hides so this needs to be replaced. The hides are 'fattened' in a drum together with beef tallow (a semi-solid animal fat). The leathers are then flattened between rollers and excess water removed.

Photo 6.3; Vegetable tanning is still carried out in open pits in many parts of the world, as in this tannery in Morocco

The hides are then air dried in an environment of controlled temperature and humidity, a process that can take four or five days, and the result is vegetable crust leather. Some type of flattening operation using a cylinder is often used.
(Continues on page 110)

An overview of the vegetable tanning process is shown here, and we are grateful to **Tärnsjö Garveri**, Sweden (www.tarnsjogarveri.com) for their kind permission to reproduce the sequence and photographs of their process.

Step 1. Swedish rawhides arrive at the tannery, pre-salted to aid preservation. (Photo 6.5)

Step 2, Liming. The hair is removed and the hides swelled using a strong alkali solution. This process is carried out in rotating drums and takes two days. (Photo 6.6)

Step 3. The hides are passed through a fleshing machine; two rotating rollers remove any remaining flesh and fat. The hides are trimmed and marked with an individual hide number to allow traceability. (Photo 6.7)

Step 4. The pH of the hides is lowered and they are treated with an enzyme which removes any unwanted proteins. Specially formulated blends of tannins are added and the tanning process, which takes several days, is carried out in the rotating drum. (Photo 6.8)

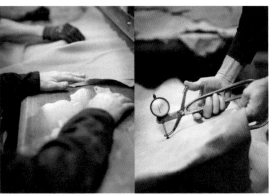

Step 5. (Right) The wet hides are pressed to remove excess water and to flatten them. They are then carefully shaved to the desired thickness. (Photo 6.9)

Step 6. The liming and tanning operations have removed the natural fats from the hides and these need to be replaced. Several methods are used including treating with fat in heated fattening mills and fattening with water soluble fats. Aniline dyestuffs are also included if required. (Photo 6.10)

Step 7. The leather is dried using a variety of methods such as hot air or by stretching on frames. Upholstery leathers are dry milled; the leathers are tumbled together and this action increases their softness. (Photo 6.11)

TÄRNSJÖ

GARVERI

HOUSE OF LEATHER

Step 8. The leathers are inspected and sorted by experienced specialists. (Photo 6.12)

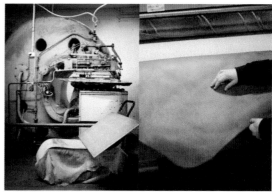

Step 9. The leathers may be finished with protective layers and water-based colours as per the requirements of the customer. Leathers may be minted - embossed with a variety of grain patterns. (Photo 6.13)

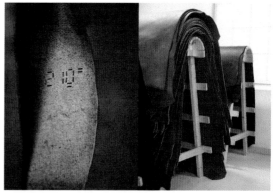

Step 10. The surface area of the graded leather is measured. Leather is sold by the square foot (ft²). (Photo 6.14)

These 'crusts' can be finished according to the customer's specification. This may involve buffing the back of the leather and spray finishing to the colour required. A final ironing operation is often involved. If a softer leather is required, the leathers can be tumbled for several hours in a rotating drum; a process known as dry milling.

Vegetable tanned leather has several useful properties. It is a firm leather that retains its shape well, but can be made softer by dry milling. It has a clean, attractive cut edge and will take an embossed pattern well. The inherent firmness is a limitation for some applications but an advantage for others, for example shoe soles. Vegetable tanned leather does not have the resistance to temperature that chrome tanned leather has (75 degrees Celsius as opposed to over 100 degrees for chrome tanned leather).

Photo 6.4; Vegetable tanned leather's firmness makes it highly suitable for quality belts

The applications for vegetable tanned leathers include furniture, (a sofa made from vegetable tanned leather sofa is a thing of beauty), footwear, bags, luggage, belts, equine leathers, book binding, shoe soling, wallets and watch straps.

Mineral tanning

This uses the salts of minerals such as chromium, zirconium and aluminium, with chromium being by far the most used.

Chromium (chrome) tanning

Chrome tanning makes use of the chemical chromium sulphate (Cr_2SO_4). The tanning takes place in acid conditions (pH 3.0 - 4.0) in specially designed rotating drums. This method promotes good penetration and a smooth, level, flexible grain in a matter of a few hours.

The chromium displaces some bound water but the main mechanism is that it is liable to form complexes of two or more chromium atoms which then form crosslinks between adjacent groups on the collagen molecules. The shrinkage and subsequent bonding of collagen molecules on drying will be impeded by the presence of these mineral salts. [4]

As the tanning process progresses, the collagen molecules combine and form thick fibrils which form the structural stability of the finished leather. These fibrils join and interweave to form fibres.

The quantity of chrome fixed is far less than is the case with vegetable tanned leather, typically three to five percent of chromium, and so the potential for shrinkage and hardening of the leather on drying is increased. For this reason oils and fats are added to the wet fibres prior to drying in a process called fatliquoring. A typical standard chrome tanned leather of the type used for footwear of clothing will contain typically five to fifteen percent oil in order to achieve the required softness.

Chrome and its use in tanning sometimes attracts bad press, and certainly there are potential hazards and environmental issues associated with the use of this chemical. This results in a lot of confusion surrounding chrome and its use as a tanning agent in leather; the main issues and the technical aspects of chromium have been explained Chapter 1 of this book, in the section The Use of Chromium (Chrome) in Leather Tanning.

Chrome tanning - an overview

The raw hide has to go through many operations, typically around 40 or so, before reaching the finished leather stage. These operations include treatment with chemicals, oils and dyestuffs, mechanical operations to remove flesh and hair, modify thickness and promote softness, and finally finishing operations to give the leather the desired aesthetic properties. The entire process can be separated into two distinct stages, **beamhouse processes** and **retanning** or **finishing**. The following is an overview of these stages, which are described in detail later in the chapter.

Beamhouse Processes

Photo 6.15; A modern beamhouse

The first stage of tannery operations is carried out in a part of the tannery named the 'beamhouse'. The origin of this term is that in the past the hides were placed on wooden beams and the fat scraped off with a curved two-handled knife. In the beamhouse the animal skins are washed, the hair is removed and the leather is pre-tanned. Pre-tanning involves a sufficient quality of tanning agent being applied to convert the animal skin into a semi-stable intermediary that can be stored for several months or transported large distances. This intermediary is called 'wet–blue' because it is still in a wet state, and reflecting the pale blue colour of the material imparted by the chrome tanning agent. The moisture content at this stage is around 25 percent; it must be kept in this condition throughout storage and transport.

The leather has not yet been dyed and, if not split, is in the original thickness (so cow skin wet-blue for example would be 5-10 millimetres thick). In principle, any leather type including nubuck, suede, aniline, pigmented, embossed, laminated, splits, etc. can be made in any colour and thickness from wet blue.

Re-tanning (finishing)

The second stage of the chrome tanning process is often referred to as re-tanning and converts the wet-blue, into usable leather. In this process, the leather is split and shaved to achieve the required thickness. Further tanning agents are added and the leather is dyed to the required colour. Oils are added in a process called fatliquoring to impart softness and a range of other properties then the leather is dried and pounded mechanically to ensure softness.
Finally finishes are applied to the surface.

While some companies do like to carry out the entire tanning process from raw-hide to finished

Photo 6.16; Automatic quality control of finished wet-blue leather after beamhouse operations

leather, many do not. Many tanneries purchase wet-blue and produce from that, thus avoiding the beamhouse operations. There are advantages to doing everything however; for example, there are several critical processes in the beamhouse which if not carried out correctly will result in poor leather. There are also commercial advantages from starting with

rawhides. But there are also some disadvantages. Buying raw hides can be a risky business - the skin is covered with hair or wool on one side and blood and fat on the other so it is not possible to evaluate the grain of the leather very easily. In the case of wet-blue, the grain is clearly visible and can be graded for quality at that stage. Also, the beamhouse processes result in a lot of effluent and waste products such as hair, salt and other chemicals which have to be disposed of. Some estimates suggest that 90 percent of waste from the tannery results from beamhouse processes.

Chrome tanning operations in detail

There follows a more detailed overview of the chrome tanning process.

Pre-treatment (Curing). To prevent the hides from rotting between the abattoir and tannery, they are cured by covering the flesh side in clean mineral salt. This prevents the bacterial action that would putrefy the skin. Other techniques are also used including chilling and the use of biocides. The salt cured (or otherwise pre-treated) raw hides are delivered to the tannery on pallets and the process of converting them to finished leather begins.

Beamhouse operations

Soaking: The hides are soaked in water to remove the salt and dung and re-hydrate them (the

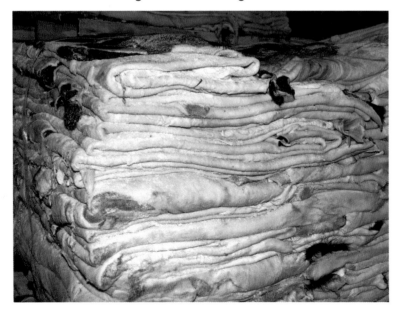

Photo 6.17; Cured rawhides awaiting processing in a tannery

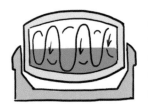

Soaking and liming operations are usually carried out in rotating drums, with slats to provide agitation

hides can lose up to 10 percent of their flayed weight).

Liming: This is a critical step in the tanning process. The purpose is to remove the hair, unwanted proteins, oil and fat, and swell the collagen fibres in the hide structure to facilitate tanning later. The hides are immersed in a strong alkaline solution and the result is that the collagen fibres swell and absorb more water. The hair swells to a lesser extent and so becomes loose and inter-fibrillary proteins become more soluble. The process, which is carried out in drums or pits, can take 16 - 60 hours. Gentle agitation speeds up the process.

Fleshing: Any flesh or connective tissue adhering to the hide is removed using a machine with bladed rollers. Any hair not removed in the liming process is also removed along with any unwanted

flesh, fat and connective tissue adhering to the flesh side of the hide.

Splitting: This operation reduces hides to the required thickness. The hides are plumped in the limed state and this is an appropriate point to split the leather into a grain layer and one or two flesh split layers. This operation is carried out by a band knife splitting machine. The edge of the hide is fed, via a grooved roller, against a sharp oscillating cutting blade.

Photo 6.19; Hides being fed into a splitting machine

Photo 6.18; Hides after soaking, liming and fleshing

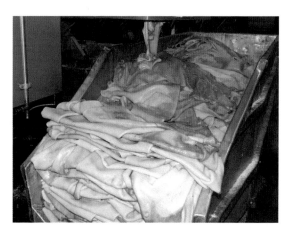

Photo 6.20; Hides after splitting and trimming

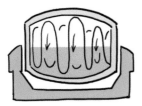

Back into drums for the remaining beamhouse operations

De-liming: Following the liming operation, the lime and other chemicals need to be removed and the pH neutralised; not to do so would result in damage to the leather. The way this is usually done is to subject the hides to a continuous flow of clean, cold water.

Bating: In this process enzymes (biological catalysts) are used to remove any unwanted inter-fibrillary proteins that will prevent the leather becoming soft, flexible and stretchy. Although in ages past animal dung was mainly used for bating, since the 1950s enzymes of bacterial origin are used. Additionally, advances in modern biochemistry have led to the increasing use of enzymes in other processes including the soaking, hair and fat removal operations. Enzymes provide a more environmentally friendly, sustainable and safer option to many traditional chemicals.

Pickling: If the hides are to be chrome tanned, the pH has to be reduced to allow penetration of the chrome. Acids are added to the hides to reduce the pH to the range 3.0 – 4.0.

Chrome Tanning: This operation converts the collagen protein fibres in the skin into a stable material that will not rot, and will maintain its properties when dry. Chrome forms crosslinks between the collagen fibres, stabilising the structure. To achieve this hides are treated in a 'liquor' of water and chrome sulphate. To ensure the tanning agents penetrate the hides they are placed in specially constructed wooden drums fitted internally with slats to provide the agitation. The drums rotate at 8 - 12 revolutions per minute and each can often contain several hundred kilograms of hides at a time.

Wet blue

In their raw state, prior to dyeing and finishing, skins tanned using chrome have a pale blue colour and are referred to as 'wet blue'. Wet blue can be described as semi-finished leather in that it is in a stable condition and is a commodity that can be shipped around the world. Bovine wet blue can be made into leather of any thickness, colour or finish. Many tanners buy in wet blue and make finished leather from this, splitting it into the required thickness, dyeing it through and applying a finish in what are collectively called 're-tanning' operations.

Photo 6.21; Author Paul examines a newly tanned wet-blue skin

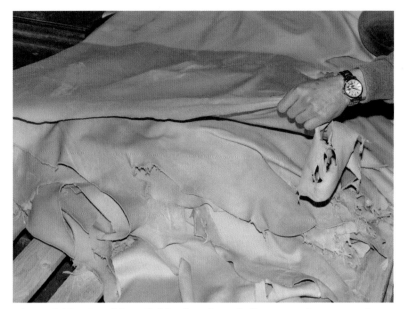

Photo 6.22; Wet-blue, finished and ready for retanning operations or sale prior to further processing elsewhere

Chrome re-tanning (finishing) operations

Splitting: Cattle leather in particular is too thick for most applications and needs splitting to the required thickness (if it has not already been done in the beamhouse). Hides over 3mm thick can be split into two or more layers. The leather

Photo 6.23; Wet-blue being fed into a shaving machine to reduce it to the required thickness

is passed through a splitting machine where an oscillating knife splits the leather to the required thickness. The grain-side splits can be processed further to manufacture the finest leathers, whilst the flesh-side splits are used to make suedes or coated leathers.

Shaving: As an alternative or addition to splitting, hides can be shaved to a specific thickness using a machine with knives mounted on a revolving cylinder.

Retanning: This is a second tanning operation the purpose of which is to further stablise the collagen network by modifying the physical properties of the leather and to aid dye penetration. The process has the effect of filling the looser, softer parts of the leather and improve the feel and 'handle'. Chrome can be used as can another tanning agents, (vegetable,

Photo 6.24; Once more, large wooden drums are employed for re-tanning, including dying and latliquoring. The fitted wooden slats provide agitation and aid penetration of the chemicals

aldehyde or syntans). The choice of the tanning agent depends on the properties required in the finished leather.

Dying: After the retanning solution is discharged from the drum, water soluble dyestuffs are added. Dying is carried out to produce leather of a consistent colour across the hide and between hides in a commercial lot.

Fatliquoring: Almost all leathers require a greater degree of softness than is obtained by tanning alone; chrome tanned leather becomes stiff when dry. Leather must be lubricated to achieve the desired product characteristics and to re-establish the fat content lost in the previous tanning operations. This can be achieved by adding oils in the form of emulsions to the leather, which coat the collagen fibres. The level of oil used (typically 3 – 15 percent based of the shaved weight), the types of oil used (animal or vegetable origin or synthetic mineral oils) and the way they are applied, have a significant effect on the properties of the finished leather. Fatliquoring is an extremely important process affecting a whole range of physical and mechanical properties of the finished leather, including strength, touch, softness, stretch, water repellence, grain tightness, and so on.

Drying: All the previous steps have been carried out in the wet state. Drying occurs when the

Traditionally, tanned leather was hung up to dry in the air. However, mechanised drying methods, which give greater control and predictability over the process, are now in common use

water in the leather evaporates into the surrounding air. With leather however, drying is quite a complicated process and the method of drying will have an effect on the softness and feel, as well as the area, thickness and even the colour of the finished leather.

Hang drying involves hanging the leather over some form of support and the leather allowed to dry naturally over a period of days. This allows the leather to shrink resulting in a soft stretchy leather.

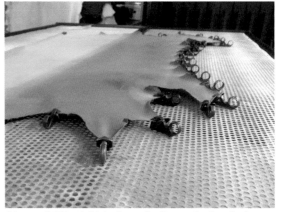

Photo 6.25; A hide 'toggled', ready for drying in an oven

Toggling involves drying under tension. The leather is secured to a heavy wire toggling frame by pegs or spring clip 'toggles' and the frame placed in an oven. This clearly speeds up the drying time but does involve additional cost. A big advantage with this method is that the surface area of the leather can be increased by several percent, an important factor as leather is sold by surface area.

Vacuum drying involves spreading out the wet leather on a heated smooth metal plate. Advantages with vacuum drying include a flat grain free from toggle marks that need to be removed. The equipment is expensive however.

Photo 6.26; A vacuum-drying machine. A hide is placed on the heated plate. The upper heated plate is lowed onto the hide and the moisture is evacuated to a highly controlled degree

After drying, the leather in this form is sometimes referred to as 'crust' and, like wet-blue, is a tradable intermediate product.

Staking: Softness can be increased by applying mechanical action during drying which separates the collagen fibres slightly. Softness can also be improved after drying by staking, either by hand – working the leather over a blunt metal blade fixed to a wooded stake (hence the name), or more usually by machine where the leather is flexed against revolving blades or forcibly passed horizontally between a series of pegs and grooves.

Shaving/Buffing: If needed, the leather is buffed in a machine using abrasive paper of varying grades, depending on the amount of material to be removed and the finish required. The leather is reduced to its final thickness and, if a suede or nubuck, until the required finish is achieved.

Finishing: Leather can be 'finished' by applying a wide range of coloured pigments, binders, waxes and resins. The purpose of finishes is to meet the requirements of the end product in terms of colour and other aesthetic requirements, feel, touch, handle and resistance to light, water, abrasion and a whole range of other characteristics. Finishes also serve to cover any non-uniformities in the leather such as colour and grain and can also mask defects.

Finishes can be applied by brushes or pads but more often they are applied by spraying. Here the finish solution is ejected from a fine nozzle by compressed air. If there is a need to hide imperfections in the leather, then pigments are added to the finish. To ensure the pigments adhere to the leather surface and form a continuous film, binders are used.

Refer to Chapter 5 for more information about leather finishes.

Photo 6.27; A spray finishing cabinet

Grading: The surface area is usually measured optically and electronically by passing the leather through a machine and the area is stamped on the hide .

Inspectors grade the leather for quality in accordance with customer requirements and specifications. For more information about leather quality and grading, refer to Chapter 7.

Photo 6.29; Substance (thickness) measurement as part of quality control and grading

Combination tanning

Approximately 85 percent of leather produced commercially is chrome tanned and 10 percent vegetable tanned. There are several variations to the processes however. Combination tanning makes use of both processes – an initial tanning stage using chrome followed by a re-tanning using vegetable tanning agents. An advantage with combination tanning is that it produces leather with the benefits provided by chrome (softness, suppleness and durability) and vegetable tanning (natural look and easy to mould).

The term 'Retan' is frequently used here, for example, vegetable or synthetic tans can be added to chrome tanned leathers to improve fullness and firmness in a process known as 'Chrome Retan'. 'Semi-Chrome' tanned leather refers to leather that has been initially vegetable tanned followed by chrome tanning in order to obtain some of the properties associated with chrome tanned leather.

Comparisons between vegetable and chrome tanned leathers

The characteristics of the two most popular tanning methods, chrome and vegetable, are summarised in the table on the following page as 'pros' and 'cons'.

We are not trying to suggest one type of leather is better than another – it all depends on the application for which it is destined. Vegetable tanned leathers are ideal for applications where a firmer, fuller leather would be an advantage, for example equine leathers, shoe soles, luggage, book-binding etc. Vegetable tanned leathers can be made softer by dry milling. Chrome tanned leathers, with their softness and drape, are ideal for garments and shoe uppers. Also, the real situation is not as black and white as the table opposite would suggest. For example, we would challenge vegetable tanning's alleged environmental credentials versus chrome, and chrome's bad press is in many instances is based on outdated information and misrepresentation of the facts.

Photo 6.28; A variety of fully finished leathers

Summarising the differences between vegetable and chrome tanned leather

Vegetable tanned leather - pros:	Vegetable tanned leather - cons:
Imagery - traditionally made using natural ingredients by skilled artisans (hand made).	Takes a long time to produce - up to 60 days.
'Environmentally friendly'.	Expensive (relative to chrome tanned).
Used for high-end luxury goods.	Can (water) stain easily.
Improves with age - develops a patena.	Limited range of colours available (light/dark, reds and browns).
Natural, rich and warm colours and tones.	Not as heat resistant as chrome tanned - can crack under direct heat.
Good for carving, embossing, moulding and shaping.	
Chrome tanned leather - pros:	**Chrome tanned leather - cons:**
Quick and easy to produce (2-3 days).	Imagery - contains chemicals (e.g. chrome) - 'bad' for the environment.
Lower cost relative to vegetable tanned.	Low skilled, mass produced.
Good stain and thermal resistance.	Heavily finished types do not have the look of natural leather.
Light weight, soft supple leathers with good drape.	
Wide range of colours and finishes possible.	

Vegetable tanned leathers do make products of great natural beauty, but so does chrome tanned aniline leather which will also develop a patina with age. Vegetable tanned leather uses natural ingredients such as tree bark and so by implication is 'organic' and more environmentally friendly than chrome tanned leather, which uses chemicals, acids and salts. However this is far from the full picture. Vegetable tanning agents are toxic if ingested and difficult to separate from the waste water and tannery sludge. The environmental impact is arguably greater as organic materials are difficult to break down.

Concerning the mass produced, low skill claim made against chrome, we can confirm that chrome tanning, especially of lightly finished leathers, does take a high level of skill, care and attention.

Chrome tanners go to considerable trouble to separate chrome from tannery waste and recycle it if possible. The consumption of vegetable tanning agents is 10 times that used in chrome tanning for a similar amount of output. One view is that the land used to grow the source of vegetable tannins would be better employed for crop production.[8] Another is that the water and energy used to produce chrome tanned leather is estimated to be 35 percent lower than that used for vegetable tanned leather.[9]

A life cycle analysis carried out by Ecobilan S.A and cited in the BLC Report 002 concluded that the three main tannages, (chrome, vegetable, aldehyde) have very similar environmental impacts. "None of the three tanning technologies under study offer a full environmental advantage over the others when considering all the key criteria that characterise the impact on the environment of these technologies".[10]

How to differentiate between vegetable and chrome tanned leather

- Feel the leather. Vegetable tanned leather tends to be firm and stiff relative to its chrome tanned equivalent, which is softer. This is not an absolute test - chrome tanned leather can be stiff and vegetable tanned leathers can be processed to increase softness.

- Burn test. Cut a thin strip of leather and ignite one end. If the leather continues burning like a glowing coal, the leather is usually chrome-tanned; veg-tanned leather will not continue to burn. After burning, rub the burned end against a white surface; chrome-tanned leather will leave a greenish ash trace, vegetable tanned leather usually leaves a black one.

- Smell it - If the leather is chrome tanned it will have a slight chemical smell. Vegetable tanned leather has a sweeter, nuttier odor. (This method is often quoted as a valid test, but we must admit that we have tried it many times with students and the results are only slightly better than chance!)

- Boil test - this is a definitive test. Place a small square of leather in boiling water for ten seconds. Vegetable tanned leather will curl and shrink significantly. On removal from the water the leather feels slippery and tannin will leach out into the water so it resembles a weak cup of tea. When cool, the leather will be darkened and hard. Chrome tanned leather remains unchanged – it does not shrink or discolour. On cooling the wet leather feels slightly clammy and if you compress it between finger and thumb, water will leech out of the cut edge.

If leather is vegetable tanned, it is quite likely to be marked as such.

Other mineral tannages

Although chromium salts are by far the most popular, other minerals are used for specialist applications.

Zirconium tanning agents are expensive. They produce a firm leather with a tight grain structure. The resulting leather is white with good light fastness. The leather has a high shrinkage temperature (90 - 95 degrees Celsius) and wash resistance. Zirconium can be used in combination with other tannages to produce a tighter grain.

Titanium tanning agents produce leathers with a tight structure and good shape retention. Combined with aluminium it gives white washable leather with a shrinkage temperature of 85 - 90 degrees Celsius.

Alum tanning is an ancient process popular in the Middle Ages. Aluminium salts combined with binders are used to produces a stable, pale leather; however the tanning agents can be washed out with water. For this reason some experts say it's not really tanning and the process has its own term – 'tawing'.[11] The leather

Photo 6.30; Cricket balls are usually made with alum tanned leather

covering cricket balls is usually alum tanned, with a tallow-based dipping for waterproofing.

Other tanning materials

Aldehyde tannages. The most common aldehyde used is glutaraldehyde; the result is soft white leather that may bleach in sunlight. The tannage is not washed out by water and can be used to produce washable leather. This type of leather is sometimes referred to as wet-white due to its colour. Applications include children's footwear and automobile leathers. Formaldehyde tanning has been phased out due to its toxicity to workers and many people are sensitive to formaldehyde. Aldehyde tanning is a modern equivalent of the ancient method of smoke tanning. The smoke from wood and green leaves, straw and the like contain aldehydes.[6]

Oil tanning is a very ancient method of tanning and traditionally cod liver oil was the tanning medium used. This is used to produce chamois (shammy) leathers from sheepskin. The leather is soft and highly water absorbent. Their main use is for wash leathers as they absorb water readily and most types of dirt are easily washed from the leather.

Chapter 6 References:

1. Richards, M. (2004). *Deerskins into Buckskins: How to tan with brains, soaps or eggs.* Backcountry Publishing.

2. Freedictionary.com, (n.d.). [Online]. *Tanning.* Available at: www.freedictionary.com. Accessed: 13/10/2014.

3. Oxford English Dictionary, 2005.

4. Sharphouse, J. H. (1983). *Leather Technicians Handbook.* Leather Producer's Association.

5. Covington, A. D. (2009). *Tanning Chemistry, the science of leather.* Cambridge: Royal Society of Leather.

6. Forbes, R. J. (1996). *Studies in Ancient Technology, Bind 6.* E.J. Brill; Leiden, The Netherlands.

7. McLean, W. (1997) [Online]. *The Manufacture of Leather – part 3.* Skin Deep. Available from: www.hewit.com. Accessed: 09/10/2013.

8. Graebin , J. (2011). [Online]. *The Environmental Impact of the Actual Tanning with Chrome or Veg.* Available at Green Cow, www.johngraebin.wordpress.com. Accessed: 01/09/2014.

9. Sorensen Leather. (n.d.). [On-line]. *Consumption of water, energy & tanning agents.* Available at: www.sorensenleather.com. Accessed: 04/02/2015.

10. All-about-leather. (n.d.). [On-line]. *The eco leather story.* Available at: www.all-about-leather.co.uk. Accessed 20/06/2015.

11. Barlee, R. (n.d.) [Online]. *The Manufacture of Leather – parts 6, 7 & 9.* Skin Deep. Available from: www.hewit.com. Accessed: 07/08/2014.

Chapter 6 Photographs:

6.1, 6.2, 6.15 - 6.28 inclusive, M G Mirams and P J McElheron, by kind permission of Ecco Shoes A/S.

6.3, 6.29, M G Mirams and P J McElheron.

6.4. Olga Popova, Dreamstime.com.

6.5 - 6.14, Tärnsjö Garveri, by kind permission.

6.30. Robyn Mackenzie, Dreamstime.com.

CHAPTER 7, LEATHER QUALITY

In this chapter we consider the 'Quality' of leather as it can be regarded differently by various stakeholders in the leather industry, and how that quality is measured. We also refer to a number of restricted substances that should never be present in leather or leather goods.

The perception of 'quality'

Leather quality can vary considerably, as does the perception of the term! What do we mean by leather quality? For a commercial leather buyer who will be using the leather to make footwear, apparel or furniture quality usually relates to the **source** of the raw hides, **utilisation** and **conformance to specifications**.

Photo 7.1; The skilled leather cutter (or 'clicker') will be able to cut components according to the quality of the material required for each

Source

The production of high quality leather depends on several pre-tannery factors. One is climate. The hides of cattle raised in cooler climates such as northern Europe are superior to the hides of cattle raised in warmer climates, due in part to the increased insect damage and resultant scratching on the hides of cattle from warmer parts of the world. The animal's diet affects its health and the condition of its hide and is therefore also an important factor. Another important issue is how the rawhides are preserved following removal from the carcass.

Utilisation

If a leather buyer purchases 10,000 square feet of leather, he would expect to use all of it. That does not mean that every single square inch is perfect. Imagine you are making shoes, the vamps are the most visible part of the shoe so clearly the leather here needs to be of a high aesthetic standard and consistent visually, free from grain difference and colour variation. Vamps would be cut from the butt region of the hide. The side pieces and heel cap are less visible so these can be cut from the neck and belly region. The tongue or linings which are largely invisible can be cut from the less visually appealing belly region. Most shoe components are skived (shaved to reduce the thickness at the edges) to obtain a smooth join between components so a skilled component cutter who is aware of the skiving tolerances can ensure that any minor defects are in the skived region.

Conformance to specifications

Commercial leather buyers will have leather specifications which describe the performance requirements relevant to a particular leather and its intended use. In practice this is a list of test requirements covering such things as:

- Leather origin, thickness, colour, grain aesthetics etc.
- Physical properties such as tear strength, flex endurance, rub and light fastness, finish adhesion etc.
- Chemical tests, pH, oil content, absence of restricted substances, etc.

Specifications should include internationally recognised methods and test requirements and be agreed on with the supplier. Many commercial leather buyers insist on test reports with each batch of leather and will carry out spot tests themselves.

Grading

Leather hides and skins traded in the market are usually graded on a scale of one to five, with one being the best material for aniline leathers for high quality shoes, garments and furniture, and five being the lowest grade for linings or parts of products that don't show. However, in the trade, the terms 'grade' and 'quality' are frequently synonymous which can be confusing for those of us who understand 'quality' to mean 'fitness for purpose'. Consider a grade-five leather, regarded as lowest quality, that could be suitable for the undersides of sofa cushions; in other words, fit for that purpose. Conversely, a grade-one leather would be too expensive for such an application, and therefore unfit for purpose!

There are in fact several grading systems in use. SATRA (formerly the Shoe and Allied Trades Research Association) proposes a grading system based on the skin's useable area, allowing for faults such as loose or fibrous areas, colour variations, brand marks, open cuts, growth marks, insect damage, scratches, etc. SATRA's system is as follows, based on the percentage of the hide that is defect-free: [1]

Leather Grade	% useable
A	100 - 96
B	95 – 91
C	90 – 86
D	85 – 81
E	80 – 76
F	75 - 71

Consumer expectations

For the average consumer of leather goods quality means appealing aesthetics and that the product is fit for purpose and doesn't develop any problems in use. With a good pair of leather shoes, one would expect the soles to wear out well before the leather upper showed any significant signs of wear. A well-constructed sofa incorporating top quality leather should last a generation or more.

Fitness for purpose - a hiker would be better off with a sturdy pair of boots rather than a gleaming pair of 'top quality' patent leather dancing shoes!

As we have seen, the production of leather is a complicated business requiring many operations where control of process times, temperatures, pH values, chemical dosages and machine settings are critical. Add to this the variations in raw materials and water quality and you can see the scope for quality variation is considerable. Sometimes, the leather quality is below an acceptable standard to a level that will cause dissatisfaction and failure in service. But here's something to consider; in all our years associated with the leather industry, we have rarely seen any leather being rejected and disposed of in a tannery - it's all used for something. The trick is, not to become the consumer that gets sold this leather in bulk form, or as garments, furniture, footwear or any other item. To avoid this, you will need knowledge of leather as a material and the ability to ask the right questions.

Generally, the best leathers are clear and supple with 'fat wrinkles' when the leather is pressed, with a 'natural' look rather than being stiff and board-like with a heavy coating of pigmentation and the look and feel of plastic.

Some tanners allow less than the optimum time to dye leather in an effort to save time and increase production. Leather that has not been

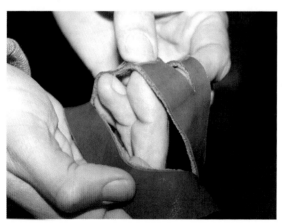

Photo 7.2; Leather that has not been dyed fully through its thickness

fully dyed through can easily be spotted by looking at a freshly-cut edge, (it has to be a freshly-cut edge as manufacturers dye the edges to hide non-dyed-through leather).

Restricted substances

Restricted (banned) substance legislation is a complicated issue. In European Union countries legislation determines the chemicals which must not be present in materials or products manufactured, imported or sold in Europe; other areas of the world have their own procedures. The reason for this is that the listed chemicals are proven (or suspected) to have, deleterious effects on health and/or the environment, from skin irritation to cancer and other serious conditions. The list of chemicals is long – several hundred, and covers a whole range of products used in the manufacture of anything, including toys, textiles and of course leather and leather goods. In the case of leather, the main restricted substances include azo dyestuffs and chromium VI (carcinogens), formaldehyde (irritant), PCPs (biocide), TBT (poisonous) and others.

Restricted substances can give problems to leather buyers, particularly when importing into the European Union from outside. (See also the section in chapter 8 on commercial leather purchase.)

Chemicals on the restricted list are, for the most part, very efficient at what they do. Azo dyestuffs are very effective at dyeing leather for example. An unscrupulous supplier may consider it cost effective to use them. While you or your customers cannot detect them, spot tests carried out by customs officials, or by consumer groups, can. This can result in fines and negative publicity. Also, one would not wish to expose users of one's product to hazardous materials.

Measuring leather characteristics

During the preceding chapters of this book we have talked much about the quality of leather and leather products, and how they can be judged particularly by their look and feel, with terms such as 'plastic looking', 'glossy', 'smooth', 'textured', etc. With leather being a natural material that goes through a number of processes to enhance its look, feel and functionality, these rather subjective judgments are very appropriate, but it is helpful to have some well-defined qualities and standards against which the characteristics of leather and leather goods can be precisely measured. For example, we can measure wear resistance and tear strength, and compare the results for a number of leathers to determine the most suitable for a range of walking boots, or measure light-fastness and finish adhesion to determine if a material is suitable for making sofas.

There are literally dozens of tests that can be applied to leather, many of which relate to national or international standards for the application for which the leather is being used. In most cases, the tests need expensive equipment and skilled engineers, technicians or scientists to carry them out, so only the largest leather manufacturing companies have the necessary laboratories in-house. Smaller manufacturers and buying organisations, as well as related trade organisations, trading standards authorities and indeed the general public have access to independent test houses at the likes of SATRA and BLC in the UK where they can carry out testing for a fee. Some of the more common tests on leather are as follows:

Rub-fastness – tests the degree to which colour rubs off the leather surface.

Light-fastness – tests fading and/or colour change due to measured exposure to light.

Water spotting – tests for resistance to staining.

Finish adhesion – tests the likelihood finishing colour to come off the surface or finshing layers delaminating.

Tear strength – tests the point at which the leather breaks when under tension.

Photo 7.3; A leather sample undergoing a tear strength test at VIA university

Looseness – tests for separation of grain and corium layers.

Tests for restricted substances – chemical tests which determine whether any of the banned substances are present in the leather.

Moisture content and **other chemical tests** that can determine the effectiveness of the tanning processes.

In addition, there is a large number of national and international standards for the manufacture of products that may include leather, each one having its own criteria for testing the components of the products. A few examples are:

The automotive industry has standards for light-fastness, rub-fastness, fogging, ageing, etc. for its seating.

The furniture and garment industries have standards for safety in the event of a fire. Although the leather itself is not likely to be a problem in a fire situation, products that it is combined with, such as linings, facings and fillings can be more problematic.

Photo 7.4; An upholstery label

Various sectors of the **footwear industry** have standards, both for whole shoes and components, with performance tests, wear tests, water penetration, etc. (We well remember a test at the ECCO shoe factory in Bredebro, Denmark, where a walking boot spent months being flexed in a walking motion under water, simulating a lifetime of fell-walking!)

The BLC in Northampton, UK, has their own series of 'Leathermark' standards for leathers, both in isolation and with respect to their suitability for various applications, and for products that are safe and comply with appropriate standards and legislation. Their members can apply for the coveted symbol to be applied to their products.

For further information about SATRA and BLC and their leather testing services, visit their web sites at:

> www.www.satra.co.uk
> www.blcleathertech.com.

Many of the points summarised above will be expanded in the next chapter when we consider dealing with the purchase of leather and leather goods on varying scales.

Chapter 7 References:

1. SATRA. (2007). *One language for leather assessment*. (Darren Brookes). SATRA Bulletin, November, 2007.

Chapter 7 Photographs:

7.1 & 7.4, Mike Mirams & Paul McElheron

7.2. Mike Mirams & Paul McElheron, with kind permission of Ecco Shoes A/S

7.3. Mike Mirams & Paul McElheron, with kind permission of VIA University

CHAPTER 8, BUYING LEATHER

With so many different types of leather and leather finishes, and the varying terms used to describe leather and its quality, the purchase of high quality leathers or leather goods may seem to be a daunting prospect! Therefore, in the following pages, we attempt to summarise the key points to consider and look for when buying leather, whether as a consumer, hobbyist or small business, or buying on a commercial scale.

A consumer's guide to buying leather

Buying leather furniture

As Valerie Knight of *The Roomplace* [1] states, leather furniture allows you to sink into luxury as the leather stretches and moulds to the shape of the body; well-crafted leather furniture provides an ideal backdrop to any room. There is also that great smell of leather – soft on the nose, luxurious, elegant and evocative.

Photo 8.1; Leather furniture - synonymous with luxury and comfort

> According to Marina Milojević´of Fragrantica,[2] leather was one of the first 'notes' in perfumery. It was the habit of the times that glovemakers in the 16th centuary would perfume their gloves with oils, including birch and musk, ambergris, juniper, certain flowers etc. and the result became associated with 'the smell of leather'. King George III was so impressed he had the royal glove makers, Creed, to make a body fragrance based on this.

Leather furniture can represent a considerable investment so it's worth doing your homework. Check on-line to view sites that specialise in the type of furniture you are looking for. Once you have done that search for a reputable furniture store, assess the scope of their selection. What do their customers say about them? Visit the store's web site, Facebook or other social media site and read what consumers are saying about the store and its products.

Visit the store and speak to their leather specialist if they have one. The larger stores will have staff with specialist leather training, although the quality of the information they impart varies from informed to misleading, hence your need to have subject knowledge. Talk to them about your requirements. If you have a young family, a white leather or aniline sofa may not be your best choice. Look at the various leather types and samples of the range of colours. Discuss the advantages and disadvantages of each. How easy are they to clean and maintain? Protective coatings are applied to some leathers to provide scratch and stain resistance to a variety of substances.

Questions to ask

Ask about the quality of the leather. In terms of bovine leathers, as previously stated, leather from animals reared in Northern Europe is regarded as being of superior quality due to feed and animal husbandry factors. Leather from North and South America is generally regarded as good value for money, although ranched animals can acquire damage to their hides and often have brand marks. Leather from Asia can vary a lot in quality - in our experience leather from animals reared in Thailand, Indonesia, and to some extent Vietnam, is more consistent than that from animals reared in China or India.

Terms discussed in previous chapters that are used particularly in respect of leather furniture are as follows.

Genuine Leather is an ambiguous term that can

The symbol indicating 'genuine leather'.

(and is sometimes meant to) confuse the consumer and calls for a degree of caution. Genuine leather is leather, that is to say, has been made from the skin of an animal, but it says nothing about the quality other than it is probably below top grain in terms of quality, possibly in strength, susceptibility to looseness and overall aesthetics. Genuine leather is usually the layer of the hide that remains after the top is split off to use for better grades of leather. The surface is usually spray-finished (pigmented) to resemble leather of a higher grade, or another animal. Cow splits can sometimes be embossed with very authentic prints to resemble ostrich, alligator, snake or lizard skin etc. We don't want to give the impression that 'genuine leather' should be avoided – far from it. Suede leather could, technically fall under the category 'genuine leather' as it does not have a grain layer but it is an excellent material for use in furniture and footwear, both functionally and aesthetically. However the buyer's quality expectations should be set in relation to what can be expected from full grain leather and, to some extent, top grain leather.

Remember, **Bonded leather** is not really leather at all, rather dust and shavings that have been bonded together. It's cheap with few of the properties associated with real leather and is not really suitable for furniture as its wear resistance and strength are poor.

Leather faced refers to furniture where the visible parts you see and sit on are made from leather; the back, the sides and the leg rests are made using inferior materials, often plastics. The label might say "Made with Full Grain Leather" which may be technically correct but can be misleading. If the price is too good to be true – it probably is. Another practice that is common with furniture is that the visible parts of the chair or sofa, as well as the parts you actually come into contact with, are made from fine quality full grain but the side panels and backs are made from less expensive finished flesh splits. This is not necessarily a problem but it's something you should be aware of.

Inspecting the leather

Is it real leather? There are several tests one can do to check if what you are examining is real leather or 'fake' made from plastic or plastic coated fabrics or non-wovens. If you can examine a cut edge you can recognise the collagen fibre structure of real leather although this is not always possible. A burn test liberates a plastic odour from fakes (and a lot of smoke); real leather does not burn easily. However most retailers have a dim view of potential customers putting a flame to a garment or sofa! An alternative simple, non-destructive test is what we call the 'finger star test'. Press the tip of your index finger into the leather depressing it a

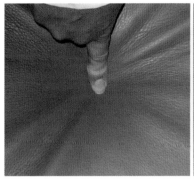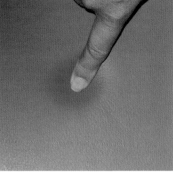

Photo 8.2; The 'finger star test' on sofa cushions, indicating real leather (left) and fake leather (right)

Smell the leather. Good leather has a clean leathery smell. If you get a rancid odour or a fishy smell this is a strong indication of poor quality leather, as cheap fish oils can be used in the production of low quality leather. Also avoid any with a chemical smell. Poor quality leather can smell of formaldehyde, a strong unpleasant chemical odour, whilst the smell of plastic materials is quite obvious.

couple of centimetres or so. Real leather reveals a characteristic star-like crease pattern as in the photograph. As the other photograph shows, fake leather does not do this. This simple test works on most leather types and works especially well on leather chairs and sofas, being good for detecting leather faced items (above). It will also work on most garments if you depress the leather with your finger into your cupped hand.

Check for high density cushions, quality stitching, and evidence of craftsmanship.

Move your hand over the leather. The material should feel supple, almost springy. It should not feel excessively stiff or papery.

Sofa construction

One way manufacturers can lower prices is by making economies in construction by using lower quality frames, foam and springs. This does of course reduce prices but long-term use will be compromised. The most durable frames are made from hardwoods such as oak or maple. Pay attention to the joints (if you can see them) which should be doweled, screwed and glued. Softer woods like pine are lower cost alternatives. More inferior still is chipboard, (particleboard or MDF), especially if held together by staples.

Now you can make an informed choice - decide on a price range. You usually get what you pay for when buying leather items.

Photo 8.3; Good quality leather cushioning should feel soft and supple to the touch

Purchasing leather garments

Leather is an ideal material for garments. In addition to protection, durability and overall aesthetics, it has a level of symbology and has achieved iconic status assisted by, amongst other things, the music and movie industries. The leather jacket has been the wardrobe essential for a range of screen heroes from Gary Cooper, James Dean, Marlon Brando, to Indiana Jones. Leather is part of the characterization of The Terminator, Lawrence Fishbourne, (The Matrix) and even Gwen Cooper, (Torchwood). [3]

A wide range of materials is used. Cowskin is the most common due to availability and price. Often with a visible grain, it is tough, durable and resistant to water and soiling and is available in a vast range of finishes and colours. Cow nappa (the term nappa denotes soft) has a smoother finish compared to cowhide. The drape is good. Bison (and similar) is rugged and durable with a textured look. Deerskin is very soft and supple yet has good durability. Goatskin is softer and

lighter than cowskin but also has good durability. Lambskin is very soft and supple, lightweight with a luxurious buttery texture, slightly stretchy feel and with good drape. It is sometimes used as a lining material.

What to look for

Firstly check out the cut of the garment. Does it 'fit' well; what about the sleeves when you extend your arms? What about the workmanship and construction? Are fastenings sturdy; do zippers move smoothly? Check the seams and stitch holes - the leather should be fully dyed through. Surface dyed leather is inferior to dyed through leather; surface dying is like painted wood – it only covers up the surface defects and colour variation. Fully dyed-through aniline leather is akin to stained wood, penetrating deep into the surface giving a more natural look. To dye leather through takes time and careful control and some tanneries take short cuts in order to reduce costs.

Check the lining - sheepskin linings provide great insulation.

In order to economise, garment manufacturers often use the highest quality leather for the most visible parts of the garment and inferior leather for the less noticeable arts, side panels, inside of collars etc. Be aware of this.

The garment should smell of leather, not of chemicals, see the section of purchasing leather furniture, above.

Photo 8.4; The classic leather jacket - always in fashion

Photo 8.5; Fine leather boots

Buying Leather Footwear

Leather footwear covers a wide range of products from lightweight sandals, through high fashion court shoes, to heavy duty hiking boots. Leather footwear should be comfortable of course and fit for the purpose it is intended for. Hiking and working boots should clearly have a more robust construction and the leather type used should be more durable than for fashion footwear.

Know your leather type; very broadly speaking good footwear is made from full grain leather, corrected grain or suede/nubuck. There are exceptions however; patent leather for dancing shoes and oil nubucks for waterproof footwear are good examples. European Union Directive 94/11 states that footwear labelled as genuine leather should be made from a minimum of 80 percent leather by surface area in the upper and lining, and the sole should contain minimum 80 per cent leather by volume.[4]

Exotic leather types should be purchased with caution – they are very expensive, and because of this, are sometimes faked! They can also have special care requirements.

The leather should be free from gouges, pit marks or open defects which could form sites for failure in use. There should be no evidence of excess glue, the stitching should be even and follow the contours of the shoe components and there should be no loose thread ends.

The colour and grain of the leather should match within the pair; components for leather footwear, especially the more visible parts like vamps, should have been cut pair-wise. Some manufacturers will attempt to 'pair up' odd shoes for example, the left shoe from one pair with the right shoe from another if the original member of the pair was rejected in production for some reason. You would expect the most visible parts of the boot or shoe, the vamp or forepart, to be made from the most appealing leather cut from the best part of the hide. It is accepted practice to use slightly less aesthetically appealing leather for the components which are less visible, such as the heel cap and tongue.

Leather footwear should always be comfortable! Aim for a snug fit. Some people buy loose fitting footwear in the belief that this will provide comfort. This is not the case with leather shoes which will eventually mould themselves to the contour of the feet, this being one of the major benefits of this material for footwear. Feet swell and get bigger as the day goes on to the extent that a shoe that fits well first thing in the morning could possibly feel uncomfortably tight at the end of the day so bear this in mind. Also, many people's left and right feet differ in size. The right foot is usually slightly bigger, and for some people, this can be up to a shoe size (6 millimetres).

Photo 8.6; Left and right shoes of a pair should match in colour and grain

Buying shoes on-line has its risks. On-line images of leather footwear will always present them in their best light with high gloss, even tight grain etc. Shoe sizes between manufacturers vary considerably; for example you might need size 44 from one brand and 45 from another. Check that the supplier offers a return/refund policy and you can change shoe sizes. As with buying other leather products or any other on-line purchase, check out the supplier's website, consumer reviews, Facebook or other social media sites.

Finally, a spot of low cost maintenance can extend the life of your footwear considerably. Remove dirt promptly and allow wet footwear to dry out. Polish and wax regularly where appropriate. Protect your new nubucks and suedes with a silicone spray and buff up with a suede reviving brush and re-treat as required.

Commercial leather purchase

In this section we will cover the leather buying needs of the hobbyist, the start-out business wishing to purchase leather goods and/or materials on a small scale, and the small to medium sized company wishing to purchase leather on a greater scale.

The story that we reproduce on the right is true, but we certainly don't want to give the impression that all leather suppliers are rogues! Far from it, we know many first class suppliers world-wide who are reliable and trustworthy, and work hard to ensure that their customers get a good deal. However, importing leather or leather goods on a commercial scale, as well as being full of possibilities for your business, can also be, as Paul's experience shows, full of potential pitfalls, some of which could seriously threaten your business. First the benefits; you can get access to good quality leather from experienced tanners at competitive prices. If you

Photo 8.7; A range of finished leathers, as might be seen at a supplier's premises

A cautionary tale directly from Author Paul's experience.

"I was recently asked by one of my ex-students, Anna, to make a presentation about leather and run a short leather quality workshop for several European sales managers from the company she had recently joined. I get asked to do this occasionally and am always happy to oblige. It's an indication that students have found the lectures useful and it keeps me in touch with what is going on in the industry.

'The company Anna had joined was a small Danish brand designing ladies high fashion leather footwear, bags and other accessories. The designs were made in Denmark, the products were produced in Asia and sold in several European regions.

'I turned up early for my session and while I was setting up for my workshop I could hear the presentation by the company's Asian leather footwear supplier who was on immediately before me. The presentation was clearly not going well and rapidly deteriorated into open confrontation between the sales managers and the supplier, with sales staff demanding explanations for what were clearly a range of leather quality related problems.

'What was interesting was the supplier's response. They refused to take responsibility for anything and attempted to bamboozle the company with false leather technology, stating such things as "Aah! It's impossible to make coloured leather with good rub fastness" and "You have chosen nubuck for that sandal - nubuck is a very weak leather". Also, when shown shoes with excessive looseness (unsightly wrinking) in the vamp, and extreme grain and colour difference in the vamps within pairs of shoes, the supplier stated that "this is a natural feature of this type of leather". (Subsequent inspection of the production numbers stamped on the inside of the tongue revealed that the shoes were not in fact cut as pairs),

'All of this was inaccurate nonsense of course as was pointed out when I got to do my session, but it caused me to reflect on what had gone so badly wrong between the Danish company and their supplier."

can develop a long-term relationship with one or more suppliers, communication becomes easier as they can get to understand your leather quality and delivery requirements and the basis is set for a relationship that is profitable for both parties. If you are buying fully or semi-finished items in the West, the labour costs in leather producing countries in Asia and South America are significantly lower than in Western Europe making this a particularly attractive option.

As for the risks, leather quality varies enormously in terms of general aesthetics, physical properties and the chemicals used to make it. Leather suppliers also vary in their technical ability, control of their tanning processes, ethical practices and ability/willingness to understand and meet your requirements.

The following problems are all too common:

- Suppliers fail to deliver leather or leather products that meet your aesthetic standards. This might involve unacceptable colour variation (either within a batch of products of even between components within a single product) or grain difference, or the leather may have loose or drawn grain or a wrinkled appearance which could rapidly develop during use. The leather may have developed waxy blooms and salt sprues, perhaps during shipping.

- Leather is frequently not 'dyed through' due to deliberate short cuts made in the tannery processes or problems of process control. This is visible at a cut edge and will be problematic if your product has raw edges or visible stitch holes.

- Problems with physical properties may include poor rub fastness, (the leather colour rubs off onto garments etc.), low tear strength or other related properties that could result in product failure in use and claims from the customer. Unless you have the appropriate testing facilities, such problems may not become apparent until products have been in use for some time.

- Finishing defects include cracking or delaminating surface finishes. In the case of suedes, the 'nap' may be uneven or appear 'too hairy'.

- Late or incomplete deliveries. While often the fault of the supplier, these can be due to lack of planning by the client, late design modifications etc.

- Presence of restricted substances. As discussed in the last chapter, certain substances must not be present in leather or present only in low prescribed limits. The challenge with restricted substances is that some suppliers may use them for reasons of cost or may just have poor controls. Their presence is not detectable visually or by touch or odour. Elaborate testing methods by specialized laboratories is required to detect them, although, as an importer, it is your responsibility to ensure that they are not present.

So the question becomes how these problems can be avoided? Clearly the choice of supplier is a major factor. We will deal with this issue and the precautions that can be put in place, depending on the size and scale of operations, to avoid the above problems in the following sections.

The hobbyist or small scale designer of leather goods

Your best choice of leather supplier will likely be a leather retailer or wholesaler, who can take the responsibility of importing appropriate quality and compliant products. These can be found in a business directory or a search on the internet. In Denmark for example we use Læderiet (www.laederiet.dk) regularly. These wholesalers typically carry a wide range of leathers often including exotic leather types. They are professional leather buyers, usually with many years of experience of the leather industry. You get exactly what you pay for, prices are reasonable and staff are knowledgeable and helpful. You can order on-line but it's a good idea to visit in person because there are often lots

Photo 8.8; Bjarne Andersen of supplier Læderet advising VIA University students.

Photo 8.9; A leather hobbyist's bench

of leathers than are not advertised on the website.

Small to medium sized enterprises

In this category we include businesses dealing in quantities of leather in the hundreds to few thousands of square feet and, or, leather items featuring collections comprising of the few dozen items to several hundred or thousands of garments, bags, gloves, footwear etc. High prices from most European sources mean that, in order to be competitive, products have to be sourced further afield. Whereas large organisations will have buying departments, used to negotiating contracts world-wide, these facilities are not normally available in-house in the smaller or medium-sized company.

Sourcing suppliers

Firstly, you need to have a grasp of the business model of most tanneries and many contracting manufacturers. Profit levels are low in tanneries, typically 5 per cent or less. They are often family owned and run, and are slow innovators. They compete on price and quality – low price usually equates to low quality although a supplier will

never tell you that! Co-author Mike has a lot of experience in sourcing suppliers and sub-contractors for European manufacturers in many fields. The following is a suggested process for new supplier selection and approval. The aim is to secure a profitable long-term relationship in the interests of both supplier and customer; this is possible, but there is no substitute for a cautious approach with procedures that protect both parties.

A model supplier selection and approval process

1. Research, research, research

Carry out some internet searches in the first instance, to see what is around, but do not rely on any web site as a measure of the company it represents. For a few dollars, any low-grade supplier can create a spectacular web site to hide behind! Respond to a few with an e-mail enquiry, initially to assess the response you get. Visit the website of a leather products association in the country you are interested in, for example the Indian Leather Products Association lists members and what they produce. Organisations in the UK such as the BLC – Leather Technology Centre and SATRA (formerly The Shoe and Allied Trades Association) have large world-wide membership and can put you in touch with possible suppliers. They can audit suppliers on your behalf though they will of course charge for this.

The business consulate or council associated with your Embassy situated in the supplier's home country can also be very helpful in putting you in touch with potential suppliers. Paul has had very good experience with the business consulate section of the Danish Embassy in India in terms of their assessing his needs and putting him in touch with credible suppliers.

Be aware of the differences in language and culture between your organisation and the organisation and country with which you are dealing. The spoken word particularly is frequently open to varying interpretations!

Relevant questions at this stage include:

- Initial commercials – could this be a commercially profitable business for both parties?

- Has the supplier a proven record of supplying international customers with leather/leather products with similar quality and quality requirements to yours? Can the supplier document this with quality records, test results, testimonials, and so on? Does the supplier have knowledge of restricted chemical legislation?

- Does the supplier have an organisation with sufficient staff skilled in relevant areas ? Can they document this with an organisation plan and CVs or biographies of key people, such as the tannery manager, technical manager, technicians, quality manager, and so on?

- Do the supplier's product range, source materials, technology used, finished leather types, etc. match your requirements? Can they provide samples and test documentation?

2. Sampling

Request some samples made to your specification from a potential supplier – we would expect relatively inexpensive items to be sampled for no cost, but be prepared to pay for large, multiple or more complex samples. Be very precise in your specifications in every detail,

so you can see how the supplier measures up when you receive the samples.

Some customers will give a supplier a sample of leather (or a product) and request the supplier to reproduce that leather, sometimes in a range of colours. However this approach can be fraught with difficulties. The 'sample' leather will have been made in a different tannery, in a different country, maybe in a different continent with different sourced material and using different water and chemicals etc. Also a supplier's interpretation of the red colour 'tomato' for example may be very different from yours! It is better to use leathers actually produced by the supplier concerned as samples, which of course will later form the basis for your quality standards. For this reason, leather or leather product buyers are advised to explain their leather quality and colour requirements to the supplier in a specification document and ask them to make samples to meet that specification – more later.

3. Visit the supplier

If the sampling proves satisfactory, be prepared to go and visit the supplier. Only then will you be able to appreciate their ability to supply in accordance with your requirements. Be extremely suspicious of a supplier who tries to put you off coming. (Mike once chased half-way around China looking for a factory that didn't exist – the supplier, who claimed to have his own factories, actually sub-contracted manufacture to whoever gave him the cheapest deal at the time!) While you are out there, visit and compare a few suppliers, and, if possible, visit a trade fair or association.

Never, never, ever place an order or sign a contract with a supplier without having approved samples and agreed specifications, prices and terms in writing. You will probably agree that this is just common sense, but you will be surprised how many people and organisations do this, tempted by the low prices and extravagant promises!

Questions that you will now need answers to (and see evidence to back them up) will include:

- How does the supplier's tannery look?
- Is there evidence of good housekeeping, chemical storage and process control throughout production?
- Is the technology modern with well-maintained equipment?
- Are workers and staff knowledgeable and well-trained?
- Is record keeping good and effective?
- Does the tannery or factory match the expectations given by the supplier's web site?

On the subject of product quality:

- Does the supplier have a documented quality management system?
- Does it have a test laboratory, or access to one?
- Do test records demonstrate consistency?
- Is the supplier's grading system compatible with your requirements?

Does the supplier have policies in place that show commitment to:

- Not use child labour?
- Provide a safe working environment?
- Protect the environment and have adequate effluent treatment facilities?

To sum up, do you have the confidence that the supplier understands your requirements and could deliver the quantities and quality that you want, when you want them?

4. Key documentation – the material and product specifications

Before production starts in earnest, all the specifications for all the products must be clearly documented and agreed by all parties, so there can be no mistake in understanding any of the requirements in the future. Effort spent at this stage is seldom wasted, as it can prevent expensive errors and misunderstandings later! Vital information to include in the specification includes, for the leather:

- Description of the material, e.g. 'Full-grain cow with light aniline finish'.
- Quantities (usually defined as square feet), and substance (thickness),
- Colours, with reference to samples or other standards,
- Grades,
- Reference to any required test results or ISO standards, etc.
- Any other requirements, such as certification, freedom from restricted substances, etc.

In addition, for made-up leather goods, it is necessary to provide reference to any drawings and/or construction specifications, and previously accepted samples, which will now become your quality standards.

A couple more points of good advice:

1. Start with small orders first; once the relationship with the supplier has started and is proving to be successful, increase the number and value of orders gradually as confidence on either side builds.

2. Avoid having all your eggs in one basket – multi-source where possible.

Smaller organisations and those without the resources or expertise to follow the above good practice in establishing a supply chain can consider using an agent to locate a supplier and source and control products on your behalf. The following illustrates the experience and capabilities of one such agent, Betty Bevan.

Betty Bevan acts as an agent/consultant for small to medium size companies looking to source leather and leather products from India and China. Betty has many years of experience working with and controlling leather quality and has lived in India.

The service she provides her clients is ensuring that their product is placed with an Indian or Chinese supplier that meets their requirements in terms of size/capacity, experience, leather type, quality, price, and so on. She will handle initial negotiations, supervise the production and quality of trial samples and first production runs, train suppliers, monitor delivery schedules, etc. She will also ensure suppliers are able to meet European Corporate Social Responsibility (CSR) requirements. Betty says her main challenges are ensuring that clients' requirements are effectively communicated to the supplier and that the supplier is willing and able to meet them consistently. To ensure this Betty looks closely at the supplier's organisation - do they have people with the required ability and experience to meet the client's standards? Do they have a record of good supplier performance? Betty also carries out supplier audits to ensure consistency. Word-of-mouth is important in the leather business and a recommendation from a trusted source can be invaluable and save you a lot of time and trouble. If you are a small to medium sized buyer, a supplier with a solid history of supplying international clients is a good starting point.

Dealing with suppliers

Once you have identified a number of potential suppliers and they have demonstrated their capabilities, the following are some pointers aimed at building a good two-way win-win relationship.

Location - products sourced from distant lands can take several weeks to reach you and there are shipping costs, check the supplier's freight policies carefully. There could be savings to be made by ordering a certain quality or combining orders. Leather goods need to be carefully packed so that problems do not occur during shipment, the appearance of mould or wax blooms on the leather can be due, at least in part to poor shipping conditions. If the nature of the business is that you may need something fast; this can be a problem with distant suppliers, and air-freight can increase the cost of the supplies disproportionately.

Finding new suppliers is time-consuming, costly and risky. When buying leather or leather products there are several advantages with a long-term supplier relationship; they get to understand your requirements and communication becomes easier. However, if deliveries arrive consistently late or damaged or with quality problems it's time to look elsewhere. Size matters. You may have more leverage if you are a significant customer of a small supplier which usually means they will be keen to provide good service. A large company is more likely to have qualified staff and better technology. You could also divide your orders between two or more suppliers, despite the potential costs, it does make you less vulnerable and provide you with more security and a back-up if things go wrong with one supplier or the other.

Don't make any unreasonable expectations of suppliers. Be realistic in terms of your delivery schedules and cautious when starting new products and leather types. Specify everything in great detail and on drawings and in text, and provide samples as standards to work to if possible. Do not rely on the spoken word! In our experience, if it is possible for something to be misunderstood, it probably will be.

Even if you are a small brand buying modest quantities of product, say a few dozen to a few hundred pairs in the case of footwear, suppliers in Asia will be interested in you. There is prestige for the supplier in supplying European or American customers as the quality and delivery requirements are usually higher. The Asian supplier can use this to get additional 'foreign' business with other brands and also secure bank loans. Western customers pay a good price and pay on time in a 'hard' currency – Pounds, Dollars or Euros. Indian suppliers have told us they can wait up to a year to get paid by local Indian buyers. Also, the Asian buyer gets intelligence in the form of Western styles, trends and tastes and some use this to develop their own designs.

Remember to select your suppliers very carefully – an organisation is only as good as its worst supplier allows it to be!

Photo 8.10; Author Mike carries out an audit at an Indian shoe factory

Chapter 8 References:

1. Knight, V. (May, 2013). *Leather living room furniture is the perfect choice for your home or office.* [On-line]. The Room Place. Available from www.furniture.theroomplace.com. Accessed 04/01/2014.

2. Milojvic M, nd [On-line] *Leather* available at www.fragrantica.co. Accessed 21/06/2015

3. Wikipedia (n.d.) [On-line] *Leather Jacket*. Available at http://en.wikipedia.org. Accessed 20/06/2015.

4. Directive 94/11/EC of the European Parliament and Council (23/03/1994), available at http://eur-lex.europa.eu. Accessed 20/06/2015

Chapter 8 Photographs:

8.1. Soloway, Dreamstime.com

8.2, 8.8 & 8.10, M G Mirams and P J McElheron

8.3. Serhiy Zamanyahre, Dreamstime.com

8.4. Sekas0906, Deamstime.com

8.5. Karam Miri, Dreamstime.com

8.6. Stocksnapper, Dreamstime.com

8.7 & 8.9. M G Mirams and P J McElhern, by kind permission of Ecco Shoes A/S

Photograph of Betty Bevan by her kind permission.

GLOSSARY OF LEATHER-RELATED TERMS

Aniline Leather: A full grain, high quality leather to which has been dyed through using aniline dyestuffs. Aniline leathers are essentially unfinished though may have a very light non-pigmented finish applied or have been lightly polished.

Aniline Plus: Aniline leather to which a very light protective coating containing micro pigments has been applied, (sometimes known as protected leather).

Antique Grain Leather: A finish achieved by applying a contrasting colour to the 'peaks' in the leather surface to the 'hollows' to produce a two tone effect which imparts an aged look to the leather.

Belly: The part of the hide from the underside of the animal.

Beamhouse: The area of the tannery where the hair is removed from hides and where the liming and fleshing processes are carried out. Before modern machinery was introduced, hides were placed over wooden beams and the flesh removed using large, curved two handled knives.

Blue, in the: (also known as wet blue): Chrome tanned hides immediately after the first chrome tanning operation.

Bonded Leather: Leather scraps can be shredded and bonded together with a latex or polyurethane binder to form flat sheets with the appearance (and smell) of leather. It's a low cost material which should not be called leather at all; durability and strength fall way below those of real leather.

Break: Wrinkling formed when the leather is folded, grain inwards with a radius that simulates the fold on the vamp that occurs when walking. Fine break (small fine wrinkles) is an indication of good quality. Course break, (fewer course wrinkles) is an indication of poor quality. Sometimes referred to as pipiness.

Buffed Leather: Leather from which the surface has been removed (buffed) by an abrasive (sandpaper) or a bladed cylinder. Leathers are often buffed on the flesh side to improve the appearance.

Butt: The part of the hide or skin covering the rump or hind part of the animal.

Bycast Leather: See laminated leather.

Cabretta: The skin of a hair sheep.

Calf Leather (skin): Leather made from the skins of young cattle from a few days to a few months old. It has a fine grain, very few defects and more supple than cow hides.

Chamois Leather: Very soft leather made from the inner side of sheep skin – usually oil tanned. It can be repeatedly washed; it has rapid water absorption and low water retention after wringing.

Chrome Retan: Leather tanned first with chrome, then re-tanned with vegetable extracts (tannin).

Chrome Tanning: The conversion of raw hides into leather using chrome (chromium) as the tanning agent. The method was introduced in the early 1900s and today approximately 85% of all leather is chrome tanned. The leathers are generally soft and flexible and available in a wide range of colours.

Collagen: The fibrous protein that makes up leather.

Combination tanning: Leather that has been tanned using two types of tanning agents, usually chrome and vegetable tanning.

Cordovan: (Shell Cordovan) is the leather made from the fibrous flat muscle beneath the hide on the rump of a horse. It has a characteristic waxy finish and very durable.

Corrected Grain Leather: Leather which had had the grain partially removed (corrected) to remove small defects and to even it out. A new surface is built used a variety of finish methods. Also known as 'Top-grain'.

Cowhide Leather: Leather made from cowhides although the term is usually extended to the hides from any bovine species.

Crust: Leather that has been tanned and dried but not yet finished. For chrome tanned leathers drying takes place after the retanning and fatliquoring operations.

Curing: The treatment of raw hides after flaying, (usually with salt) to retard bacterial attack and putrefaction.

Deliming: Following liming the alkali is removed and the pH is reduced prior to the bating operation.

Drum Dying: Dyestuffs are added to leather and water and the mixture tumbled in a drum for several hours. This process allows the dyes to fully penetrate the leather.

Embossed Leather: Leather, usually corrected grain or splits to which a pattern has been pressed into the surface. This embossing may make one leather type, say cow, appear to be another animal type, like lizard or alligator, or imitate full grain leather.

Fatliquor (ing): An emulsion of oil in water, used to lubricate the leather fibres and modify a whole range of physical properties.

Finish: A mixture of dyes, pigments binders and other materials applied to the grain or sometimes split surface of leather to protect it, mask imperfections, increase utilisation or impart aesthetic characteristics.

Fleshing: A mechanical operation usually involving bladed rollers that removes any flesh, fat or muscle adhering to the flesh side of the hides.

Full Grain Leather: Leather with the grain layer fully intact - not having been corrected or altered. Aniline and semi-aniline leather are referred to as full-grain leathers.

Glazed leather: Aniline leather with the surface polished under some pressure using an agate stone, or a steel or glass surface. The result is a shiny, glazed surface that may have a varnish applied. Use on cow leathers and chrome tanned kid skins, also kangaroo.

Grain (surface): The outside surface of a hide or skin which if untreated shows the natural characteristics of the leather, pores , wrinkles, etc. The grain surface is characteristic for different species of animals.

Hide: The outer covering (skin) of a large animal – cattle, ox, horse, etc. Also the leather made from such an animal – cowhide, ox hide, horsehide etc. Pelts from smaller animals, sheep, goat etc. are referred to as skins.

Kips or Kipskin: Hides from a bovine animal that is between the size of a calf and a mature animal.

Laminated Leather: Leather to which a surface layer of typically polyurethane foil has been applied for visual effect or wear resistance, waterproofing, etc. Many lower grade leathers can be as the basis for laminated leather.

Leather: The general term for a hide or skin that has its original fibre structure intact and has been treated stabilise the structure so that it is flexible and imputrescible.

Liming: The process carried out early on in the tanning process in strongly alkaline conditions prepares the hides for the tanning process by removing the hair and swelling the hide to facilitate the uptake of chemicals later.

Metalized leather: leather with a metallic lustre – achieved by the application of a metal foil.

Milled (grain) leather: leather that has been dry milled in a drum. The tumbling action enhances the natural micro pebble-like effect and softens the leather. Can be used for both chrome and vegetable tanned leathers.

Mineral Tanned: Leather tanned with compounds of mineral origin. Chrome is the most used mineral. Other examples include aluminium and zirconium.

Nap: A soft or fuzzy surface, such as with nubuck or suede.

Nappa: Originally used to describe soft full grain sheep, kid or lamb skin but the term has been extended to include soft cow skin.

Nubuck: Leather with the grain surface lightly buffed to produce a fine 'nap'.

Oil Tanned: Leather tanned with oils, usually of a mineral origin.

Patent leather: Leather with one surface covered with a flexible waterproof film with a mirror-like surface. Leather coated with a plastic film less than 0.15 mm thick can be classified as patent leather. Also known as laminated leather or bi-cast.

Patina: A lustre or sheen that develops on certain leathers, (vegetable tanned and aniline leathers) with use and over time. It's a form of exotic darkening and is the leather's reaction to oxidation, light, oil, dirt and aging generally.

Perforated leather: Leather which has been perforated with small holes. It is sometimes used by auto leather manufacturers in an effort to aid airflow and seat ventilation.

pH Scale: A measure of hydrogen ion concentration. A solution of pH 7 is regarded as neutral. Lower numbers indicate increasing acidity; higher numbers indicate increasing alkalinity. Several tanning operations are pH dependant.

Pigmented Leather: A full grain leather to which a pigmented polymer finish has been applied to cover defects, increase uniformity and provide protection. It can also be made from split leather.

Printed Leather: Leather with a surface pattern produced by embossing or other techniques such as screen printing.

Pull-up Leather: Also referred to as oil pull-up leather. Leather treated with oils and waxes so that when it is folded or stretched, it becomes lighter in colour at the stressed area.

Quebracho: A vegetable tanning agent extracted from the bark wood of a South American tree. The tree has a hard heavy wood – *quebar hacha* means 'the hatchet breaks'.

Raw Hide: A hide, as removed from the animal but may have been treated, (with salt) to preserve it prior to tanning.

Retan: A secondary tannage, different to the primary tannage.

Semi-aniline Leather: A full grain leather to which has a light pigmented finish has been applied to impart a degree of colour uniformity and offer a degree of protection against fading, staining etc.

Side: Half of a whole hide, cut longitudinally.

Snuffing: The leather is abraded with brushes or fine sandpaper to remove the grain, either to correct defects or to produce a fine nap on the surface of the leather, (nubuck).

Split Leather: Leather resulting from the splitting process where leather is split from the grain layer into two or more layers to produce a grain split and a flesh split, (with thicker hides also a middle split). Split leather may have a pigmented polymer finish applied and then embossed. Alternatively the surface may be buffed to produce a suede.

Splitting: Cutting leather into two or more layers.

Square foot (Ft²): Leather area is often quoted and is sold by the square foot. There are 10.76 square feet in a square metre.

Suede: Leather that has been finished by buffing the flesh side to produce a nap.

Suede split: Leather from a flesh split that has been buffed, usually on the split surface to produce a nap.

Tanning: The process which converts raw hides into finished leather.

Tawing: This is an old English term which refers to converting animal skins into leather using alum (the mineral aluminium potassium sulphate). It produces a white, stiff leather.

Top-grain Leather: Leather to which the grain layer has been lightly treated, by buffing or sanding, to remove defects and imperfections. A pigmented polymer finish is then applied. An artificial grain may be embossed into the surface. Also known as corrected grain leather, it is often used to make pigmented leather.

Upholstry Leather: Leather used for furniture, seating and automobile applications. Mostly from cowhides, top grain spits go to make high quality, flesh splits for lower quality.

Vegetable Tanning: The conversion of raw hides into finished leather using tannin extracted from trees and plants as the tanning agent.

Wet Blue: Leather which has been chrome tanned but not processed further. It's sold packed in this wet state.

Wet White: Semi-finished leather tanned using organic compounds.

Split Leather: Leather resulting from the mechanical splitting process where layers are split from the upper grain layer. Two layers are produced from thinner leathers, a 'grain split' and a 'flesh split', whilst thicker hides can produce a 'middle split' also. Flesh and middle splits may have a pigmented polymer finish applied and then embossed. Alternatively the surface may be buffed to produce a suede.

INDEX

Aldehyde tanning — 121
Alligator leather — 72-74
Alum tanning — 120
Aniline leather — 87, **88-89**
Animal rights — 27
Animal welfare — 26-29, 64, 65-66, 68, 71-72, 73, 76, 80
Antique leather — 98
Anthropodermic bibliopegy — 81-82

Bating — 42-43, 114, **114**
Beamhouse — 111
Beamhouse operations — 112-114
Bevan, Betty — 142
Biofabrication — 18
Bonded leather — 100
Bovine leather — 53-55
Brain tanning — 38, 103
Buffing — 117
Buyers guide, leather — 131-142
Buying leather footwear — 135-136
Buying leather furniture — 131-133
Buying leather garments — 134

Camel leather — 67
Chicken leather (skin) — 68-69
Chrome (chromium) — 25-26
Chrome tanning — 45, **110-117**, 114
Chrome tanning & vegetable tanning compared — 118-120
Collagen — 40, 51-52, 104, 105-106
Combination tanning — 118
Cordovan — 64
Corium — 54, 55
Corfam, (DuPont), leather substitute — 25-26
Consumer expectations — 126
Corrected-grain leather — 88, 93

Crocodile leather (skin) — 72-74
Crocodile leather (fake) — 74
Crust — 117
Curing — 112

Deer leather (skin) — 66-67
De-liming — 114
Dry milled leather — 97
Drying — 116-117
Dying — 116

Eel skin — 80
Embossed leather — 74, 95-96
Enzymes (use in tanning) — 108, 114
Evans, Mark (etched leather art work) — 20
Exotic leathers — 63-83

Fake leather, tests for — 132-133
Fast fashion — 29-30
Fatliquoring — 116
Finishes — 46, 74, **87-100**,
Finishing — 46, 47, 111, 117
Fish skin — 76-81
Fleshing — 113
Frog skin — 75-76
Full-grain leather — 87, 100

Genuine leather — 132
Glazed leather (finish) — 100
Global leather industry — 31-32
Goat leather — 57-59
Grading — 117, 126-127

Horse leather — 63-64
Human leather — 81-82

Kangaroo leather — 64-66
Kappel, Janne (artist) — 20

Laminated leather — 98-99
Leather, applications — 18-20

Leather, as a bi-product of
    the meat industry 15
Leather characteristics 128-129
Leather, commercial purchase 136-138
Leather, conformance to
    specification 126
Leather, consumer
    expectations 126-127
Leather, buying – consumers
    guide to 131-136
Leather, definitions 14
Leather, environmental impact 22
Leather faced 132
Leather finishes 87 - 100
Leather buying, hobbyist 138-139
Leather naturally 22-25
Leather origins 37-40
Leather quality 32, 125, 126
Leather, real or fake? 132-133
Leather, the smell of 16, 131
Leather's structure 51-60
Leather, substitutes 16
Leather testing 128, 129
Leather, uniqueness of 16
Levi, Kobi (footwear designer) 20
Liming 108, 113
Lines of tightness 52
Lizard skin 72

Marks & Spencer 29
Medieval tanning methods 41 - 43
Metalised leather 100
Milled leather 97

Nappa 134
Native Americans, leather
    making 38
Neanderthals 39
Nubuck 95

Oil Pull-up leather 96-97
Oil tanning 121
Qstrich leather 67-68
Otzi (The Iceman) 13-14

Parchment, & vellum 44
Patent leather 99
Patina 88
Perforated leather 100
Pickling 114
Pig leather 59-60
Pigmented leather (finish) **91-92**, 100
Printed leather 100
Product specifications 141-142
Pull-up leather 96-97

Rawhides 108, 111
Restricted substances 127.128
Re-tanning 111-112, 115-
    116, 118
RSPCA, recommendations 28-29

Semi-aniline leather (finish) 90-91
Shagreen 79, 80
Sharkskin 80-81
Sheep leather 55-57
Shrunken heads 82-83
Snake skin 69-72
Shagreen 79
Shaving 115, 117
Softex, (Toyota) 17
Split leather 45-46, 55, 88,
    93
Splitting 113, 115
Staking 117
Stingray skin (shagreen) 79
Suede 58, 59,94
Supplier selection 139-143
Syntans 46

Tannin 43, 106
Tanning, process 40-41, **104 –**
    121
Tanning process,
    do-it-yourself methods 78, 103
Tanning, medieval methods 41-44
Tannery business model 32-33
Tawing 120
Titanium tanning 120

Toad skin	75-76
Toggling	116
Top-grain leather	87, 100
Vegetable tanning	43-45, **106-110**
Vegetable tanning & chrome tanning compared	118-120
Wet blue	111, 114
Wet white	121
World Animal Protection (ranking)	27-28
World's first prosthetic	40
World's oldest shoe, Areni-1	39
Zirconium tanning	120

20011204R00086

Printed in Great Britain
by Amazon